Tax Shelters — The Basics
1985 Edition

Arthur Andersen & Co.

HARPER & ROW, PUBLISHERS, *New York*
Cambridge, Philadelphia, San Francisco, London
Mexico City, São Paulo, Singapore, Sydney
1817

Acknowledgment

Arthur Andersen & Co. professionals are taught the benefits of using teamwork throughout their careers. It is no surprise, then, that this book results from the combined efforts of many of my colleagues from a number of Arthur Andersen & Co. offices. They know who they are and they require no specific acknowledgment from me. They probably would say anyway that it was all in a day's work.

Leonard Podolin
Chicago, Illinois

Library of Congress Catalog Card Number 84-48134

Printed in the United States of America

Contents

This book will not guide an investor to a *particular* tax shelter investment, nor will it lead him to the *right* one. It is not intended to. Its purpose is to make the potential investor knowledgeable enough about tax shelters to recognize among the many that are offered those that are legitimate investment opportunities and to recognize also when professional advice and counsel are needed. In doing so, tax shelters are neither championed nor condemned; they are simply explained.

Preface

Since publication of the first edition of this book in 1983, significant events and tax law changes have affected many aspects of tax shelters. For example:

□ The government has aggressively used its powers to enjoin the sale of abusive tax shelters and to impose penalties on those who sell such investments.

□ The IRS has implemented a nationwide program of notifying investors in abusive shelters, prior to filing their returns, that claimed deductions and credits will be disallowed and that penalties may be assessed.

□ Certain tax shelter offerings are now required to be registered with the IRS when they are offered to the public.

□ New tax legislation has further tightened the rules under which the benefits of shelter investments are determined.

□ Tax shelter offerings have begun to place more emphasis on income, and less on deductions.

There is no sign that the pace of such change will slow; more likely, it will quicken. For example, there is a ground swell of sentiment for a simpler, more equitable income tax system that has found expression in proposed legislation for a "flat tax" or a "fair tax." There is also some support for proposals to adopt a consumption tax that would replace the present income tax system, or a value added tax that would supplement it.

What does all this mean for tax shelters that are structured to take advantage of existing investment incentives? Will shelters become relics of the past? Or will they simply be restructured to take advantage of any new law, whatever that may be? And how complex and equitable will be the rules that serve to move existing investments through the transition to any new system?

Only time will tell. But in the meantime, shelter investors and their advisers should keep abreast of proposed legislation that may affect the tax results of their investments. And prospective investors need to determine how current law affects any proposed investment *before* signing up.

The second edition of *Tax Shelters — The Basics* reflects relevant tax rules as of October 31, 1984.

Introduction

It is only because the term "tax shelters" is so easily recognized and so widely accepted by investors that it is used to refer to the subject matter of this book. The term is unfortunate because it suggests that the sole purpose of such investments is to seek shelter from income taxes — and never mind the economics of the transaction. Such a narrow view of these investments is unwarranted and it will remain so until our top income tax rate exceeds 100%. Fortunately, that is unlikely.

So-called tax shelter investments exist only because they are encouraged by our income tax laws. The provisions that foster them did not become law through caprice or inadvertence; they were adopted because Congress believed they would advance a national purpose. That purpose was to encourage investment in those sectors of our economy that needed additional capital to achieve certain economic and social (and perhaps political) objectives. Such targeted investment required greater encouragement than the usual incentives that move capital from individual savings to business investment. Special inducements were required that would provide capital *formation* for business while allowing capital *retention* by individual investors. The tax provisions on which legitimate tax shelter transactions are based provide those inducements.

Investors who are willing to commit risk capital to those investments our lawmakers have sought to encourage are granted certain tax advantages. Those advantages take a number of forms — immediate deduction of certain costs, rapid recovery of others, tax credits, etc. They are available not only to those who are active in the business in which they invest, but also to passive investors willing to supply the necessary capital. In making such investments, however, an investor must realize that these tax provisions can only *enhance* the economic viability of an investment and alone cannot *provide* economic substance to a transaction that lacks that viability absent its tax benefits.

Most passive investors have neither the time nor the expertise required to shape an investment vehicle to yield those special tax advantages that are available as incentives to investment. A more important handicap is the inability — from lack of special knowledge, experience, contacts or whatever else — to structure an investment that is also economically feasible when measured against the essential investment tests of risk and reward.

It becomes necessary then for others to make investment opportunities available and they have done so with zeal. As a consequence, investors have been deluged with opportunities from tax shelter promoters to invest in office buildings, apartment houses, warehouses, shopping centers, post offices, boxcars, fishing boats, airplanes, computers, oil and gas drilling rigs, farms, orchards, vineyards, cattle, timber, coal, oil, gas, gold, silver, precious stones, movies, plays, cable television, lithographs, master recordings, books and countless other investments, including even bibles.

Perhaps it was inevitable that in such a spate of opportunity some of the investments lacked economic substance; that some failed to measure up to the accepted standards of an "investment"; that the only advantage many of them offered was their purported tax benefits; that some of them resulted in the total loss of the amount invested; that some may cause economic and tax adversity for years to come. The deficiencies in many of these investments will, unfortunately, become even clearer to some investors as the Internal Revenue Service pursues its intention to closely monitor tax shelter investments, particularly those it perceives as "abusive."

When they are properly structured, properly marketed and properly executed, tax shelters can be a legitimate investment opportunity for the high-bracket taxpayer who is willing to assume a greater-than-average risk to achieve a greater-than-average potential investment return. Those who are willing to assume those risks, however, often lack even the general knowledge of the "ins and outs" of tax shelter investments that is essential to determine whether such an investment is appropriate to their circumstances and needs. This book is especially intended for those investors.

Included first in this book is a discussion of the basic issues that determine whether a shelter proposition is also a true investment opportunity. Next is a discussion of the special tax attributes, good and bad, that are shared by most shelter investments. Specific types of shelters are then discussed, with emphasis on their particular tax advantages and their potential tax detriments. In referring to these chapters that deal with specific types of shelter investments, the reader should recall that the matters discussed in Chapters 1 and 2 are essential to a full understanding of the subsequent chapters. Finally, there is a glossary of terms often encountered by tax shelter investors and appendices containing selected information that may be helpful to the reader.

This book will not guide an investor to a *particular* tax shelter investment, nor will it lead an investor to the *right* one. It is not intended to. Its purpose is to make the potential investor knowledgeable enough about tax shelters to recognize among the many that are offered those that are legitimate investment opportunities, and to recognize also when professional advice and counsel are needed. In doing so, tax shelters are neither championed nor condemned; they are simply explained. The explanation of the tax benefits of shelters is concerned only with legitimate shelters and not with those that abuse the tax laws on which they are based. An investor who enters into a shelter transaction that legitimately accomplishes its tax objectives can do so with the knowledge that the investor is doing nothing that is suspect under our tax laws. What the distinguished jurist Learned Hand said almost 50 years ago is no less true today:

> Any one may so arrange his affairs that his taxes shall be as low as possible; he is not bound to choose that pattern which will best pay the Treasury; there is not even a patriotic duty to increase one's taxes.

The discussions in this book of the tax results of shelter transactions are based on federal tax rules. State and local tax laws, however, also may significantly affect the tax results of shelter investments. Since state and local tax rules in many cases differ from the federal rules, it is particularly important that they be considered before entering into a tax shelter transaction.

Chapter 1

The Basics

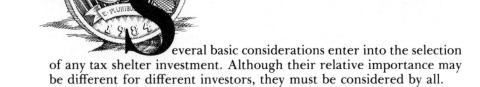

everal basic considerations enter into the selection of any tax shelter investment. Although their relative importance may be different for different investors, they must be considered by all.

The Emotions of Tax Shelter

The term "tax shelter" often elicits a strong reaction from those who encounter it. To some, a tax shelter is a giveaway device designed to enrich the high-bracket taxpayer at the expense of the "average" taxpayer. It is a gimmick, a loophole, a proof of Mr. Bumble's assertion that "the law is a ass."

To others, a tax shelter is a panacea for all tax problems, to be sought at almost any cost. Its rewards are sure, since they have been attested to by friends, relatives, business associates and other seekers of equity under confiscatory tax laws. It is a status symbol of sorts, used only by the truly discerning investor worldly enough to appreciate it in its many forms.

In reality, and in fairness, a tax shelter is neither of these. A tax shelter is nothing more than an investment that has been structured to yield the maximum tax benefit from certain provisions incorporated into tax law to achieve specific purposes. Whether those purposes are to encourage specific types of investment, to achieve a social goal or to cater to the demands of so-called special interests is irrelevant to the investment decision. The incentives are there to be used. They are based on law and are not meant to be measured against standards of fairness or morality. The judgment of a tax shelter must be based on its economic viability as an investment, not on its acceptance as socially desirable.

From the standpoint of the investor, there should be no "emotions" of tax shelter. Tax shelters are legitimate investments that are unique because of their tax benefits. They should be judged on that basis.

What Is a Tax Shelter?

Since an understanding of tax shelter investments begins with understanding what the term means, it may be helpful to examine the components of the term.

The word "tax" needs little defining. Everyone knows what a tax is and accepts it, however unwillingly, as one of the two certainties of life. We know too that a "shelter" is something that protects or shields. Although it is natural to think first of a shelter as a means of protection from the elements, it also may be something that protects capital from erosion by eliminating or deferring a tax that would otherwise diminish that capital.

The word "investment" is more difficult to define, but perhaps a workable definition is this:

> An investment is an outlay of money (or credit) for something that will produce current and recurring income during its holding and/or a future gain on its disposition. (For purposes of this definition, it is assumed that the requirement for the production of current income can be met partially through the reduction of a current expense — such as a tax.)

An investment also involves an assumption of risk — the acceptance of the possibility that the expected benefits may not be realized and that the amount invested may be partially or wholly lost. The degree of risk inherent in an investment is ordinarily (but not always) commensurate with the amount of the potential reward.

Putting the pieces together, the following definition of a tax shelter investment evolves:

> A tax shelter investment is an outlay of funds at risk to acquire something of value, with the expec-tation that its holding will produce income and reduce or defer taxes and its ultimate disposition will result in the realization of gain.

Who Should Invest in a Tax Shelter?

Tax shelters are not for everyone. The first criterion for such investments is that the investor be subject to a high marginal income tax bracket. Although this ordinarily means the 50% bracket or thereabout, each investor must individually decide if a particular bracket is sufficient to yield the required tax benefits from the investment. But those who meet that basic criterion are not necessarily suited to tax shelters, particularly if they are not risk-takers. Even the confirmed risk-taker should not invest without clear and certain knowledge of what a tax shelter is. This requirement for information includes a general knowledge of shelters — including their structure and operation, their tax benefits, their risks, their disadvantages, etc. — and very specific knowledge of any shelter being considered for investment.

In summary, then, an investor in a tax shelter should be a high-bracket risk-taker willing to spend the time and effort required to form a considered judgment about whether a particular investment is suited to the *individual's* specific tax and investment positions and their effect on family financial objectives.

What Tax Results Should a Tax Shelter Achieve?

If a tax shelter investment is to achieve the tax objectives for which it was created, it must provide one or more of the following results.

Deferral of Tax

The aim of many tax shelter investments (perhaps most) is to defer the payment of taxes that otherwise would be due now. This objective can be accomplished in a number of ways, but the net result of any of those means is the creation of initial tax losses that approach or, in some cases, exceed the investor's initial cash investment. From a tax standpoint, these losses must be *bona fide* and able to withstand scrutiny by the Internal Revenue Service. This requirement usually presents no serious problem for legitimate, investment-grade tax shelters, since they do not achieve their results through illusion or legerdemain.

Permanent Reduction of Tax

Just as a tax can be deferred, it can be reduced permanently. Some tax shelters offer this incentive in addition to tax losses that defer taxes. One way permanent reduction of tax is accomplished is by means of credits against a tax that otherwise would be due. Once earned, these credits generally are permanent; but under certain circumstances, they may be partially or wholly forfeited later. In a properly structured tax shelter, such forfeiture should only occur (if at all) through action of the investor, not through disallowance of the transaction that created the credit.

Creation of Income Taxable at Favorable Rates

Tax rates are discriminating in their application. They discriminate not only among *levels* of income but also among *types* of income. Most types of income are subject to maximum tax rates, the actual rate depending on the level of that income. Some types of income are not taxed at all. Between those extremes is a type of income that enjoys the special status of duality — partly taxable and partly not. That income is the much sought-after long-term capital gain, 60% of which is excludable from income in determining a taxpayer's regular tax liability. (But see the discussion of the alternative minimum tax on page 23.) A tax shelter investment that ultimately results in the realization of long-term capital gain by its investors is rightly considered a successful one. The degree of that success, however, depends on the amount of the gain relative to the cost of the asset that created it.

Capital gain can derive from two sources. It can arise through appreciation in value, which may represent a real value increment or merely the result of inflation. Such gain also can arise because the tax basis in the asset sold has been reduced by depreciation and other deductions. If these deductions have been used to reduce income that would have been subject to the highest tax rates, their return as capital gain obviously is of great benefit. The chances of achieving this result today are limited, however, and the investor who does so is twice-blessed.

Tax-Exempt Income

Some income is exempt from tax, most notably the interest income realized from obligations of state and local governments (municipal bonds). In a sense, these investments are the ultimate shelters, since income from them is entirely free of federal tax. However, they do not provide losses to offset ordinary income, as many other shelters do, nor do they generally offer the same opportunity for appreciation in value.

The Risk Factor

No investment is without risk, and tax shelters are no exception. Although tax shelters are risky, some are riskier than others. One of the most trying challenges in constructing a tax shelter investment program is the assessment of risk. Many factors enter into that assessment, some of them imponderable. Even so, an investor ultimately must respond to the insistent voice that asks "Is the probable economic return on this investment commensurate with the risks you are taking?" In answering that question, an investor might consider the following.

The Source

An investor ordinarily doesn't happen upon a tax shelter opportunity; someone usually brings it to the investor's attention. In such case, an investor should realize that a fee or commission probably will be paid in connection with the sale of the investment. Since the investment's recommendation does not usually come from a disinterested party, the investor must trust the sales agent's professional competence and integrity. This ordinarily poses no practical problem, since many shelter investments are offered by established brokerage houses and other reputable sales organizations. An investor should be particularly careful, however, of solicitations by "cold calls," long-distance telephone, or any "boiler room" method. Legitimate tax shelter investments normally are not marketed that way.

The Type

Tax shelter investments generally are of two types, which may be described loosely as either public or private offerings. Public offerings are those that have been registered with the Securities and Exchange Commission or with a state agency for intrastate sale. They are accompanied by a statutory prospectus or offering circular that explains the proposed investment in considerable detail.

Private offerings are not registered with any federal or state agency. Such investments may be offered only to a limited number of sophisticated investors who meet certain income and net worth requirements. These offerings are accompanied by a private placement memorandum that describes the proposed investment and furnishes the information that investors need to make an informed investment decision.

The registration process for a tax shelter offering is expensive and investors normally must bear the costs. This is not necessarily a negative factor, however, since the completeness and thoroughness of the disclosures required in a public offering may well justify the additional cost.

Any tax shelter investment opportunity (other than a straightforward investment such as municipal bonds) that does not come to an investor in one of these ways should be viewed with caution or avoided entirely.

Who Is the Promoter?

The Dutch tulip craze did not happen spontaneously. The "tulipomania" that gripped Holland in the 1630s and sent the price of a single tulip bulb rocketing to the equivalent of several thousand dollars resulted from the active promotion — to the point of hysteria — of an investment that ultimately brought ruin to many. Just as this historical disaster had its advocates, every tax shelter investment has its promoter or sponsor. This does not suggest that that there is any relationship between tax shelters and the tulip fiasco. But it does demonstrate the need for practical values and credible promotion in tax shelter investments. The success of a tax shelter investment often hinges on the integrity, knowledge and experience of its promoter.

An investor can learn much about the promoter by reading the prospectus or the private placement memorandum. It usually is appropriate to make further inquiries through banking, brokerage, credits and industry sources. Although such careful checking requires time and effort, it is necessary. An investor should remember that there are more important criteria than "face value" in judging the credentials of a tax shelter investment promoter.

What Is the Investment?

Every investor in a tax shelter should carefully consider what type of an investment is being entered into. Ideally, the shelter should be a type of investment the investor knows something about, even if that knowledge is only general. An investor should be wary of "new" deals, "never been done before" proposals. Although all such opportunities are not suspect, the risk in tax shelters probably increases in proportion to their novelty. Therefore, an investor's understanding of the transaction is essential.

The Operator's Compensation

Investors cannot expect those who manage and operate tax shelter investments to undertake that task without compensation. To preclude any later misunderstanding, however, an investor should know how and to what extent compensation will be paid.

Compensation can be paid in various ways. Some of it may be paid from the investors' original capital contributions (and some shelters are heavily "loaded" with this cost), some from subsequent operating income, and some by "carrying" the operator through assigment of an equity interest disproportionate to the operator's investment. Regardless of how and to what extent compensation is paid, the investor must be satisfied that these costs are reasonable.

The Smell Test

Some tests of the efficacy of a tax shelter can be rather basic; this test is one of those. Some tax shelters may simply "smell" bad because they are offensive to reason. In assessing any tax shelter proposal, an investor should closely consider if the investment makes sense. Most people have a "gut reaction" to their initial contact with almost everything, and this reaction probably is right more times than not. If the transaction promises a ratio of first-year tax deductions to initial cash investment that seems "too good to be true," an investor should be instantly on guard, because what seems "too good" may well be, so, for example, such investments may require investors to assume personal liabilities well beyond their initial investment. There's nothing inherently wrong with this, and some perfectly legitimate shelters are structured to achieve multiple writeoffs through the use of debt. In such case, investors must realize that they are assuming actual personal obligations and are not getting a "free ride."

The Gimlet Eye

The Internal Revenue Service has more than a passing interest in tax shelter programs; its interest abides. Unless a tax shelter is a straightforward, run-of-the-mill type of transaction with clear tax results, it stands a good chance of being closely inspected by tax examiners. These examiners normally are not amateurs, nor are they generally known for their compassion and tolerance of the follies of man.

While many criteria are used in selecting tax returns for examination, it probably is safe to say that investment in a tax shelter will increase the chance that a taxpayer's return will be audited by the Internal Revenue Service. The new emphasis the IRS is placing on ferreting out such transactions for scrutiny, the continuing efforts by Congress to close perceived "loopholes," and the new penalty provisions (discussed in Chapter 2) lend weight to that conclusion. Taxpayers who formerly were sportingly willing to play the "audit lottery" may now find themselves engaged instead in a game of Russian roulette. Accordingly, an investor in a tax shelter should be reasonably sure that the anticipated tax benefits are based on a reasonable interpretation of tax law. A tax shelter offering may include either a ruling from the IRS or an opinion of a qualified tax professional on the tax consequences of the transaction. Absent these, the offering should contain a thorough and professional discussion of the tax issues and their risks. Whichever of these is included, it should not be taken lightly. The investor should read it, note what it says (and doesn't say) and understand it; if necessary, the investor should consult a qualified tax adviser.

Investors also should understand that recent developments in audit procedures may inhibit their ability to fight their own battles and make their own deals with the Internal Revenue Service. In the past, the IRS was required to examine a partner's individual return in order to propose adjustments originating from changes to a partnership return. Under procedures recently adopted, a partnership's designated "tax matters partner" may agree to changes to the partnership return that will bind all the partners. These rules are complex and there are exceptions to them; an investor should realize, however, that participation in a tax shelter partnership may diminish the ability to deal independently in the investor's own tax affairs.

Loss of Tax Benefits

It is of vital importance that a tax shelter investment yield the tax benefits it promises. Although the offering memorandum or prospectus should include a professional tax adviser's opinion on the tax aspects of the venture, the Internal Revenue Service is not bound to the same conclusions. Practically speaking, only a ruling from the IRS itself can bind it and then only if all material facts were disclosed to the IRS in the ruling process. Thus, an investor cannot be *certain* of the IRS position on the tax results of a shelter investment until it has been reviewed in the IRS examination process. In some cases, this may culminate in litigation. Because of that, an investor must be willing to place great confidence in the tax opinion of the experts; if those experts are unknown to the investor, it may be prudent to check their conclusions with the investor's tax adviser.

Tax benefits can be lost for various reasons, such as lack of a profit motive, lack of economic substance, or failure to meet the statutory at-risk requirements. Losses also may be deferred from one year to a subsequent period if the earlier deduction distorts income. These factors are discussed in Chapter 2.

Man Bites Dog

Things happen every day that seem to defy reason or accepted standards of conduct. Tax shelters can be like that; they can eventually yield results contrary to those for which they were created. When this happens, the financial results can be disastrous. How this can happen is discussed later (see page 19), but it is one of those elements of risk that an investor must consider in assessing the desirability of a tax shelter investment.

Additional Investment

The amount originally invested in a tax shelter may not represent the investor's total commitment to the venture. In some cases, payment for the investment is staged — payable over a period of years; in others, the additional commitment may be tentative and perhaps represented by a letter of credit that the investor is required to obtain from a bank. Each of these arrangements is an acceptable means of financing the initial and subsequent financial requirements of a venture. However, an investor who enters into such an arrangement must realize that this results in an enforceable commitment beyond the original cash investment; such an investor must be willing and able to discharge that commitment when it comes due.

Tax Rates

Income tax rates are an important factor in assessing the desirability of a tax shelter, for they determine the extent to which the investor will derive benefits from initial tax losses and incur tax liabilities from future taxable ordinary income and capital gains. Although tax rates are most often thought of as a factor in measuring the anticipated return on a tax shelter investment, they must also be considered in measuring its risk. The reason for this is that tax rates are not stable; they may change in response to economic or political conditions. Accordingly, an investor who enters a tax shelter with the expectation of using deductions arising from this investment at a 50% tax rate must consider whether that rate can reasonably be expected to apply during the probable term of the investment. Not only *may* rates change, but the income levels to which those rates apply *will* change, at least over the near term. For example, married taxpayers who file a joint return for 1984 will be subject to the 50% rate when the couple's taxable income exceeds $162,400. For 1985, as a result of indexing tax brackets for changes in the Consumer Price Index, the 50% applies to the couple's income over $169,020. For 1986 and thereafter, just when the couple will be subject to the 50% rates in each year will not be known until late in the preceding year when the indexed tax rate schedules are published. In addition, an investor's own income level may add uncertainty to figuring any future tax bracket, since future income levels may not be readily predictable.

The Rewards

After assessing the risks of a tax shelter, an investor must assess the potential rewards. Like any other investment, a good tax shelter must offer an economic return that is commensurate with its risks. This is difficult to evaluate, for the risks generally are more certain than the rewards. But the rewards too can be reasonably weighed and a balance struck.

The rewards of a tax shelter investment are projected from many factors. Ultimately they depend on the accuracy of assumptions about such factors as the availability and use of tax losses and tax credits; the generation of minimum amounts of gross income; the incurring of certain levels of expense, including carrying charges; the costs of amortizing loans; the level of future interest rates; the level of future tax rates; the residual values of assets; and others.

None of these factors can be predicted with certainty, but the assumptions on which they are based can be assessed for reasonableness. If they pass that scrutiny, then the value of the rewards can be measured quantitatively by several tests, such as discounting future cash flows to their present value or computing an internal rate of return.

What Is the Rate of Return?

In theory, the rate of return on an investment should be a simple matter, for all the investor usually wants to know is "How much am I making on my investment?" Unfortunately, the answer to that deceptively simple question is not so easy and may involve concepts and computations that leave the investor feeling something like the anonymous person who lamented some 400 years ago:

Multiplication is vexation,
Division is as bad;
The Rule of three doth puzzle me,
And Practice drives me mad.

Computing the rate of return on a tax shelter investment need not be that trying an exercise, although there is more than one method of doing so and no absolutely preferable method. A tax shelter investor should be aware of the two most commonly used methods, however, for the investor must have some means of comparing the return from a tax shelter with the return from a "safe" investment. That is the only way the investor can determine whether the shelter investment offers a return that is commensurate with its risks. In the final analysis, a tax shelter investment must offer a better potential rate of return than available alternative investments of comparable risk.

One method of evaluating the return on a shelter investment is the internal rate of return (IRR). The IRR is the rate at which the sum of the discounted cash flows — both positive and negative flows — is zero. Another method, the present value method, uses a fixed discount rate to compute the present value of the future cash flows from the shelter investment. Each of these approaches is explained more fully in Chapter 12. More important for now is that the investor knows that such tests can be (and must be) made before that critical equation can be completed and, if all goes well, balanced:

Reward = Risk

The Common Threads

here are common threads that run through the fabric of most tax shelter investments. Before examining the unique features of the more common types of tax shelters available today, it may be helpful first to examine those tax attributes that are common to most shelters. It should not be surprising to most investors that these common threads, which are woven together in the creation of tax shelters, are sometimes good and sometimes bad.

The Good Things

Perhaps it is natural to seek first the good and to leave the bad for last. The following discussion covers those attributes of tax shelter investments that allow them to yield the tax results sought by investors.

Limited Partnership Form

Most tax shelter investments are structured as limited partnerships in which the investors are the limited partners. There are compelling reasons for this that override any other considerations. (Certain negative aspects of the partnership form of organization are discussed later.)

Availability of tax benefits. A partnership is not itself a taxable entity under tax law; the tax results of a partnership's operations flow through the partnership to the partners. Thus, ordinary operating losses of a partnership are treated as ordinary deductions by the partners; capital gains realized by a partnership are treated as such by the partners; tax credits earned by a partnership are claimed as credits by the partners, etc. The partners then account for their shares of such income, loss or credits in their own tax returns, which may add to or reduce their tax liabilities. As a consequence of this treatment of the partnership's tax results, subsequent distribution of profits by the partnership to its partners generally can be made without tax consequences to the partners. This treatment is in marked contrast to the tax results of operating as a corporation, which is a taxable entity separate from its stockholders. A corporation must itself pay tax on its income and must itself use (or lose) its losses and credits. Its dividend distributions to stockholders are taxable to them, even though the income from which the dividend was paid

13

was taxed at the corporate level. Thus, the corporate form of business organization results in the "double taxation" for which it is so often criticized; the partnership form does not.

Special allocations. One advantage of the limited partnership is the opportunity it affords for special allocations of tax attributes among certain partners or classes of partners. Thus, partnership losses and cash flow may be allocated disproportionately to limited partners until they have received amounts designated by the partnership agreement. Specific tax deductions and credits may also be allocated to the partners who pay the costs from which those items arose.

These special allocations of partnership items cannot be made indiscriminately; they, as all partnership allocations, must have "substantial economic effect." They must actually affect the dollar amount of the partners' shares of the total partnership income or loss, independently of tax consequences.

Although *special* allocations of tax attributes are allowed under the partnership form, *retroactive* allocations are not. Accordingly, an investor who joins a partnership late in the taxable year cannot share in the partnership losses for the full year.

The association problem. Although it is critical to the success of most shelter investments that they be treated as partnerships for tax purposes, one of the tax risks of a partnership investment is that the partnership will be treated (and taxable) as a corporation rather than as a partnership. This can happen when a partnership agreement contains provisions that bestow on the partnership too many of the characteristics commonly found in a corporation; in such case the partnership will be considered an "association," which is taxable as a corporation.

Although an investor cannot be certain that a partnership will be treated as such for tax purposes, the investor usually can be reasonably assured of that result from information contained in the prospectus or offering memorandum.

A tax shelter offering frequently includes a ruling from the Internal Revenue Service or an opinion of a tax professional on various tax matters that affect the investors. One of those is the qualification of the entity as a partnership for tax purposes. The ruling or opinion ordinarily will discuss in some detail those characteristics that determine tax status and should conclude that the entity will be treated as a partnership for tax purposes.

A tax opinion is only as good as the firm that expresses it. It would be prudent for an investor to determine, perhaps through a tax adviser, that the opinion on the tax status of the venture was rendered by a reputable firm with experience and expertise sufficient to warrant confidence in its advice. As additional assurance, an investor may also ask a tax adviser to review the opinion contained in the offering. This review cannot be done without incurring some cost, but it may well be worth the price if it affords greater confidence to the investor.

Limited liability. A very important benefit of operating in the limited partnership form is that it allows the limited or passive partners to place a ceiling on their exposure to financial loss. That ceiling generally is the amount of the limited partners' investment in the partnership (and any additional amounts they may be obligated to contribute); any exposure to risk of loss that exceeds that amount is borne by the general partner.

Twice limited. A limited partner is limited in more ways than one. Not only is such a partner's financial liability limited, but so too is the participation in the partnership's operations. Although a partner need not be mute, a limited partner normally is expected to be relatively quiet. A limited partner does not ordinarily participate in the day-to-day affairs of the partnership. Such a partner does not set employees' salaries, or prescribe tenants' lease terms, or negotiate with lenders, or decide where to drill the next oil well, or drive a company car. Thus, an investor who participates in a tax shelter through a limited partnership should not expect to become actively involved in the management of the venture, for such an investor will not.

The general partner. The key to unlocking the potential for success in a tax shelter partnership is the general partner. It should be the fervent hope of the limited partners that the key fits.

The general partner is often the one who conceived and promoted the investment opportunity on which the partnership is based. Clearly, the general partner should know the partnership's business well. This industry knowledge is essential, since the general partner will be the principal decision-maker for the venture. If the venture is to succeed, those decisions must be the right ones. The general partner's decisions will affect not only day-to-day activities of the partnership but perhaps also the partnership's success in ultimately disposing of its assets at the most favorable price.

In view of the general partner's critical role in the success or failure of a tax shelter investment, an investor should learn as much as possible about this key figure. This includes the general partner's reputation in the industry, details of prior experience and success in managing similar ventures, and any other information the investor believes is relevant to the investment decision. Although most of this information ordinarily will be included in the prospectus or offering memorandum, an investor may want to make independent inquiries to verify the details with other sources.

Related parties. A tax shelter limited partnership is seldom self-sufficient for all its needs. It will be necessary to contract with third parties for certain goods and services. This is not exceptional and the general partner should be capable of handling such transactions as a matter of course. It happens sometimes, however, that these third-party contractors are related in some way to the general partner (or may even be the general partner). This does not necessarily mean that the transaction is suspect; there are times when such a relationship may even be desirable.

It is essential to the orderly operation of a limited partnership that the limited partners realize that related-party transactions sometimes occur. When they do, the limited partners should determine that the terms of the transactions are reasonable.

How can a limited partner know whether related-party transactions exist? Ideally, the general partner should fully disclose such arrangements. If a limited partner is unsure about such transactions, the partner should simply ask.

Conflicts of interest. A conflict of interest exists when a person's private interests conflict with the responsibilities imposed on the person by a position of trust. Related-party transactions can pose such a conflict between the private interests of a general partner and the general partner's obligations to the limited partners. Although the potential for such conflicts generally is disclosed in the prospectus or offering memorandum, such disclosure does not necessarily resolve all potential problems. Accordingly, an investor must have enough confidence in the integrity of the general partner to believe that conflicts will be resolved equitably. This sometimes may require an exemplary display of confidence, since some general partners may be engaged in personal business transactions or in the management of competing partnerships or properties that create substantial potential for conflicts of interest.

Financial and tax information. Every limited partner needs both financial and tax information on the results of the partnership's operations. Such information should be routinely supplied by the general partner. If a tax shelter is registered with the Internal Revenue Service (see page 28), the registration number should be supplied to the limited partner at or near the time the investment is made.

Tax information on a limited partner's distributive share of partnership income, loss, credits and other items, is an absolute necessity. This information (called a Form K-1) should be provided on a timely basis each year to ensure that it can be included in a partner's individual income tax return without interference with normal filing practices. The partnership tax information received by a limited partner should not come as a surprise, since the general partner should have furnished estimates of the distributive shares of income or loss for use in the limited partner's personal tax planning. The final tax results of the venture's operations should reasonably approximate these earlier estimates.

During the course of each year, the general partner should furnish limited partners with periodic financial information on the results of the venture's operations, along with comments on significant items. This information can be very useful to a limited partner, for it permits comparison of actual results with those that were anticipated in the financial projections on which the limited partner based the decision to participate in the venture. If actual results are significantly less than those projections, this may signal an unanticipated problem that requires some action to get the venture back on track. Although a limited partner expects and welcomes *tax* losses in the early years of a venture, there is no comfort to be found in *economic* losses.

In addition to more frequent periodic financial information, a general partner should furnish the limited partners with annual statements covering the results of operations. These statements generally should be audited, although there may be situations where unaudited statements are sufficient. Such reporting requirements are ordinarily covered in the partnership agreement.

A limited partner should carefully review the financial and tax information provided, seeking to understand all the relevant details. If the partner has questions or needs help in interpreting the information, it may be prudent to consult financial and tax advisers.

S Corporations

An S corporation is a special type of corporation that, by election, is treated in its tax results somewhat like a partnership. Thus, it can be used as a shelter investment vehicle to achieve for its stockholders much of the tax flow-through results that the partnership form of organization achieves for partners. Although generally not as flexible as a partnership in operations and results, the S corporation's attributes have been improved by recent changes in the tax law. For that reason, an S corporation may, under the proper circumstances, be a viable tax shelter vehicle.

Depreciation

The tax losses generated by many tax shelter investments are attributable principally to deductions for depreciation. Depreciation is a noncash charge against income that is allowed by tax law to enable an investor to recover the cost of a depreciable asset over a period of time.

The period of time over which the cost of an asset may be depreciated depends on the nature of the asset. Under present depreciation policy (the Accelerated Cost Recovery System [ACRS] adopted in 1981), the period for most depreciable real property is 18 years (15 years both for property placed in service before March 16, 1984, and for low-income residential property); for most tangible personal property, such as machinery and equipment, it is five years. Land, of course, is not depreciable.

The method used to determine annual depreciation under ACRS depends on the nature of the asset; it is usually an accelerated depreciation method. That method permits recovery of the cost of an asset at a rate that exceeds ratable or straight-line recovery of cost. For example, the undepreciated cost of real property with an 18-year depreciable life is recoverable at a rate equal to 175% of the rate that would allow straight-line recovery over 18 years. The cost of tangible personal property generally is recoverable through use of a rate equal to 150% of the straight-line rate; the actual recovery rate used in determining the annual allowable depreciation is fixed by statute and varies depending on the property's recovery period. (ACRS cost recovery tables for personal and real property are provided as Appendix A, B and C.) Straight-line depreciation may also be used, at the option of the taxpayer.

Depreciation deductions thus are vital to most tax shelter investments. The combination of short depreciable lives and accelerated rates of recovery often produce substantial tax losses in the early years of a tax shelter that contribute significantly to its overall economic viability to an investor. (As discussed in Chapter 4, however, it is not always advantageous to use accelerated depreciation.)

Tax Credits

Another tax attribute that is shared by many tax shelter investments is tax credits. These credits, direct reductions in income taxes otherwise due, are an example of the use of tax policy to achieve economic goals. They are an incentive to encourage investment in certain types of property and thus serve to stimulate economic growth.

Investment tax credit. The most common credit now available is the investment tax credit allowed for investment in most business personal property. The credit is either 6% or 10% of the cost of qualifying assets, the rate depending on the asset's depreciable life under the ACRS depreciation rules. The investment credit arising from some tax shelter investment programs, particularly leasing transactions, can be significant. However, qualification of property for the investment credit is subject to certain at-risk rules that are discussed later.

Although the investment tax credit is a significant tax incentive to investment, it is not free. The credit exacts a cost because it requires that the depreciable basis of the asset on which it is earned be reduced by one-half the amount of the credit.

Alternatively, a lesser credit may be claimed (8% or 4% rather than 10% or 6%), in which case no reduction of basis is required.

Rehabilitation credit. Much discussion in recent years has concerned the desirability both of recycling older buildings for modern use and of preserving structures of historic significance. To induce taxpayers to participate in those conversion and preservation efforts, the law allows substantial tax credits.

For rehabilitation of industrial and commercial buildings that are at least 30 years old, a tax credit of 15% of the rehabilitation costs is allowed; the credit rises to 20% for costs incurred in rehabilitating buildings that are at least 40 years old. A more liberal credit of 25% is allowed for costs incurred in the rehabilitation of certified historic structures, including those that are residential property.

Like the investment tax credit, the rehabilitation tax credit exacts a cost from those who earn it. Except for a certified historic structure, the tax basis of property on which the rehabilitation credit is claimed must be reduced by the amount of the credit. For a certified historic structure, the required basis reduction is one-half the amount of the credit. (No basis reduction is required for credits on certified historic structures placed in service prior to 1983, and transitional rules will exempt from the reduction requirement certain structures placed in service as late as 1985.)

Rehabilitation expenditures, including those incurred for certified historic structures, are ineligible for the accelerated depreciation method of cost recovery. Their cost must be depreciated under the straight-line method — recovered ratably over the period (18 years) prescribed by the ACRS system.

The rehabilitation tax credit is discussed in more detail on page 44.

And the Bad

Other common attributes of tax shelter investments must be considered by an investor. Although these items generally can reduce the economic benefits of tax shelters, they do not necessarily affect all shelters. Some of these items are simply inherent in the investment, some do not apply to a shelter unless some action is taken by the investor to bring them into play, and some have no effect without the presence of other circumstances in an investor's personal tax position.

Recapture

Some of the benefits derived from tax shelter investments may be forfeited upon their disposition. Other benefits are conditional when granted; if a taxpayer later does not meet those conditions, the benefit must be forfeited or returned in whole or in part.

Tax credits. Tax credits — both the investment credit and the rehabilitation credit — are conditional incentives to investment. They are granted under the condition that the property investments from which they arise are to be held by an investor for specified minimum periods of time. Disposition of the property prior to the expiration of the required period results in the restitution or "recapture" of all or part of the credit, depending on the time period for which the property was actually held. The amounts recaptured are added to the investor's tax liability for the year of disposition.

Investment tax credits claimed on property under the at-risk rules (discussed later) also are subject to recapture. That recapture may be caused either by early disposition of the property or by lapse of adherence to the at-risk requirements.

Depreciation. Like tax credits, depreciation also can be "recaptured." Unlike the recapture of tax credits, depreciation recapture does not result in the creation of tax obligations *per se*, although its effect can be much the same. Depreciation recapture recasts the tax nature of a gain realized from the disposition of depreciable property. Gain that otherwise would be a capital gain taxable to an individual at a maximum rate of 20% is recharacterized as ordinary income, subject to rates as high as 50%. Thus, depreciation previously claimed that has reduced the tax cost of the asset must be recaptured or restored before capital gain can be recognized.

Like many tax rules, the rules that require depreciation recapture do not apply evenhandedly to all depreciable property. Depending on the circumstances, depreciation may be required to be recaptured:

☐ Entirely.

☐ Only to the extent that it has exceeded straight-line depreciation.

☐ Not at all.

The first category of recapture applies generally to personal property and nonresidential real property depreciated under the ACRS rules.

The second category applies to residential real estate. The third category applies to real estate (nonresidential and residential) on which a taxpayer has elected or is required to recover costs under the straight-line (ratable recovery) method of depreciation.

Where real or personal property is disposed of in an installment sale, all depreciation recapture amounts are recognized as ordinary income in the year of sale, regardless of the payments actually received in that year.

Turnaround or Crossover

A perfectly legitimate tax shelter can carry with it a potential for disaster. This threat — commonly known as *turnaround, crossover* or *burnout* — usually is defined as that point in time when an investment begins to generate taxable income that exceeds its cash flow. This occurs generally because the investment has yielded the lion's share of its depreciation allowances, the noncash charges that previously created tax losses, while its debt reduction costs — a cash charge that is not a tax deduction — continue on.

This event should not catch a tax shelter investor unaware, since it should have been anticipated from the financial projections originally provided to the investor and/or through subsequent updates of those projections. With proper planning, an investor should be prepared to cope with turnaround when it occurs.

The potential shock of turnaround can be avoided in a number of ways. An obvious shock absorber could be created early, through cautious investment of the tax savings generated by the investment for use later to pay post-crossover taxes. For reasons known only to themselves (and perhaps it's only human nature or reluctance to accept the inevitable), few investors follow this course.

Another possible solution — the "treadmill" approach — is investment in another tax shelter in order to take advantage of early losses for shielding the income from a turnaround shelter. This too is an obvious solution, but it is one that should be planned well in advance. It should not be grasped as a last-minute solution to a crossover problem, since such a hasty approach to tax shelter investments can create more problems than it solves.

Disposition

Ideally, the disposition of a particular tax shelter should occur only as a result of a voluntary action precipitated by events over which the shelter's managers have control. One happy example of this is a sale of the property at the optimum time at the optimum price. Unfortunately, that does not always happen. Some shelters suffer a premature demise under circumstances that amount to a salvage operation under unfavorable conditions. This can happen when the operation of a debt-financed investment becomes economically unfeasible, perhaps because it was ill-conceived in the first place or because it fell victim to changes in economics, demographics or other conditions. In such case, creditors may move swiftly to protect their own interests.

The most favorable results to an investor under those circumstances may be the opportunity to walk away with nothing, to write off the investment to experience and call it quits. But tax laws are not so forgiving; they require, for example, a reckoning at that point for tax credits that are not fully earned. Should there be debt on property that exceeds its tax basis, the law may construe the transaction as a "sale" of the property that results in taxable income, most or all of which may be ordinary income from depreciation recapture. An investor may incur a substantial tax obligation without the receipt of any cash with which to pay it.

Even an orderly disposition of a tax shelter investment can yield negative results through recapture of tax credits or depreciation. In such case, however, the investor may receive some "real" consideration (cash) to pay tax obligations arising from the disposition. Whether the disposition arises voluntarily or involuntarily, an investor should be prepared through proper planning to cope with the financial results.

Gifts and bequests. A tax shelter investment can be disposed of through gift or bequest. In the case of gifts, however, the donor must be wary of the tax results. Whether such gifts are charitable or noncharitable, they may sometimes generate adverse tax consequences, particularly where debt on the property transferred exceeds its tax basis. Bequests normally do not pose that problem, since the property attains a new tax basis, measured by fair market value, upon the death of the owner. That ultimate solution to the problem, however, can be described only as extreme.

Interest Expense Limitations

Interest expense can be a significant cost in any tax shelter project where acquisition of the venture assets is heavily leveraged through the use of debt. Financing through debt is common, for example, in the real estate industry.

Interest costs generally are deductible in determining taxable income, and such costs contribute significantly to the tax losses generated by many tax shelter investments. The interest expense incurred to acquire or carry property held for investment, however, cannot be deducted without limitation. Except for interest incurred on a home mortgage and other solely personal interest charges, investors are allowed to deduct freely only $10,000; investment interest in excess of $10,000 can be deducted only if an investor has net investment income to cover or offset it. Net investment income includes dividends, interest, rents, royalties, short-term capital gains, and certain recapture income realized from disposing of investment property. Investment interest on property subject to a net lease may also be reduced to the extent of the excess of certain expenses incurred over the rental income from the property.

An investor in a tax shelter should determine at the outset the tax status of any interest costs that are to be incurred. Often those costs are deductible without limitation because the venture is engaged in the active conduct of a trade or business. Investments that *appear* to involve the active conduct of a trade or business sometimes may be classified as passive investments on which the deduction of interest is limited. Should this happen, the investor should determine if there is sufficient investment income to allow the interest deduction.

The deduction of interest expense may also be limited if the debt is incurred to purchase short-term obligations sold at a discount. The amount of interest allowed to be deducted is calculated by determining the daily portions of the acquisition discount for each day the obligation is held. This prevents, to a certain extent, the "front-loading" of interest deductions and matches the time of interest expense more closely with that of related interest income.

The interest expense will eventually be completely allowed as a deduction. Investment interest that is not deductible in the year incurred can be carried over for deduction in subsequent years, again subject to the limitation. Even if such interest costs are ultimately used as deductions, they lose some of their value due to the time lag between their incurrence as cash outlays and their use to reduce taxes. (Taxes saved in a later year are worth less than those saved in an earlier year because of the time value of money.)

At-Risk Limitations

A true investment involves an exposure to risk. Generally this exposure to risk determines the economic return on an investment; an investment with little risk ordinarily offers no great promise of reward. In recognition of that basic investment maxim, Congress has done everything it can to assure that the risks of tax shelter investments are at least commensurate with the rewards they offer.

Losses. Generally, an investor in a tax shelter that generates tax losses must be at risk on the investment in order to use those losses to reduce taxable income. Thus, the investor must be willing:

☐ To commit personal funds to the venture's activities, or

☐ To be personally liable for debt incurred by the venture in carrying on its activities, or

☐ To pledge property not employed in the activity to secure debt incurred in carrying on the activity.

If an investor's loss from an activity exceeds the total of these amounts, the excess loss cannot be deducted. Initially qualifying to use losses, however, does not permanently secure them. Subsequent changes in an investor's at-risk position can cause previously allowed losses to be recaptured and returned to income. The reverse is also true; an investor who is denied losses under the at-risk rules can later retrieve those losses by increasing the amount at risk.

There is one significant exception to the at-risk rules, for which many tax shelter investments, by their nature, qualify. The at-risk provisions do not apply to investments in real property. Thus, such property can be acquired by the use of debt that is secured only by the property itself; there need be no personal liability by the investor to secure the use of losses. (Exception to the at-risk rules is also provided for certain closely held corporations actively engaged in equipment leasing; this is discussed in Chapter 6.)

Tax credits. An investor generally cannot earn investment tax credits on property for which the investor is not at risk. Like the at-risk rules that limit losses, the investment credit at-risk rules require that the investor be at risk through the investment of personal funds or through the personal liability for debt. There is, however, an important and relatively liberal exception to this general rule. So long as an investor is at risk for at least 20% of the cost of investment credit property, the full cost of the property may qualify for the investment credit, but only if the remainder of the cost is provided by certain qualified lenders, such as governments and unrelated financial institutions. (See page 77 for further discussion of these rules.)

Once qualified under the at-risk rules, an investor in property on which the investment credit was claimed must remain so; if the amount at risk later decreases, a proportionate part of the property's original cost is disqualified for credit. On the other hand, an investor who initially was denied an investment credit because of the at-risk rules may subsequently earn that credit if the investor becomes at risk.

Alternative Minimum Tax (The Law Giveth and the Law Taketh Away)

In many ways, the tax laws are generous to those who invest in legitimate tax shelters. Whatever its source, however, generosity usually is not unbounded. Thus, Congress has ensured that no investor gets too much of a good thing. This has been accomplished by providing that certain taxpayers who have little or no taxable income under normal tax rules must pay an alternative minimum tax (AMT).

The extent to which a taxpayer incurs an alternative minimum tax depends on the extent to which certain tax deductions, identified as "tax preferences," have been used to reduce the taxpayer's regular tax liability. Thus, what our tax laws give with one hand is taken away with the other.

The AMT employs a complex scheme of taxation. The base on which the tax is imposed is "alternative minimum taxable income" (AMTI). The starting point for determining AMTI is the taxpayer's adjusted gross income, which is then adjusted as follows:

☐ Increased by the amount of certain tax preference items and any net operating loss,

☐ Decreased by the amount of certain "alternative tax itemized deductions" and any "alternative tax net operating loss," and

☐ Reduced by an exemption amount ($40,000 for joint returns, $30,000 for unmarried taxpayers or $20,000 for married taxpayers filing separately).

The resulting AMTI is subject to a tax rate of 20%; if that amount (reduced by certain foreign tax credits) exceeds the tax determined under the regular tax method (reduced by foreign tax credits and other credits), the taxpayer must pay the excess in addition to the regular tax.

The tax preferences included in determining AMTI generally are the following:

☐ The long-term capital gain deduction (the 60% of such gains that is excluded from the regular tax base).

☐ Accelerated depreciation in excess of straight-line depreciation on real property not subject to ACRS depreciation.

☐ Accelerated depreciation in excess of straight-line depreciation on leased personal property not subject to ACRS depreciation.

☐ Accelerated amortization in excess of regular depreciation on pollution control facilities.

☐ Excess of intangible drilling costs (as defined) over the net income from oil and gas properties.

☐ Excess of percentage depletion over the adjusted basis of mines, oil and gas wells, and other natural deposits.

☐ Excess of depreciation allowed on certain "recovery property" (15- and 18-year real property and leased personal property depreciated under the ACRS rules) over depreciation that would have been allowed using the straight-line method over prescribed "recovery periods."

☐ Excluded dividends.

☐ Bargain element of incentive stock options (i.e., the excess of the fair market value of the stock over the option price when the option is exercised; this does not apply if the optioned stock is sold within a year of exercise.)

☐ Excess deductions for mining exploration and development (the excess of the deduction over ratable amortization over 10 years).

☐ Excess deductions for magazine circulation expenditures (the excess of the deduction over ratable amortization over three years).

☐ Excess deductions for research and experimental expenditures (the excess of the deduction over ratable amortization over 10 years).

For expenditures in the last three categories, taxpayers can avoid incurring a tax preference item by electing to amortize such costs over 10 years (three years for magazine circulation expenditures) rather than currently deducting them in full.

Intangible drilling costs also are given special treatment under the AMT rules. Such costs are qualified expenditures also subject to the 10-year amortization election. More significant, however, is the election available to individuals who incur those costs directly (not as limited partners). They may elect, for wells located in the United States, to capitalize the costs and recover them by using accelerated cost recovery allowances over a five-year period. This election serves both to remove those costs from the preference status and to qualify the costs for the investment tax credit.

The alternative tax itemized deductions that may be used to decrease AMTI are *only* the following personal deductions:

☐ Medical deductions and certain losses,

☐ Charitable contributions,

☐ Qualified housing interest,

☐ Other interest expense,

☐ Estate tax on income in respect of a decedent

In determining the allowable amounts of these deductions, the following special rules must be considered:

☐ The medical deduction must be adjusted to reflect a 10% base, rather than the 5% nondeductible base used for regular income tax purposes.

☐ Only casualty, theft and wagering losses are allowed as deductions.

☐ Qualified housing interest includes (generally but not exclusively) interest on debt incurred to acquire, construct or substantially rehabilitate property that is the taxpayer's principal residence or is a qualified dwelling (house, apartment, condominium or mobile home used by the taxpayer during the taxable year).

☐ Other interest expense is allowed as a deduction only to the extent of "qualified net investment income." This limitation is basically the same as that presently used in determining the allowable deduction for investment interest expense, except that all net capital gains (not just short-term gains) are treated as investment income, as is the dividend preference item. Losses from limited business interests (tax shelters and others) must also be taken into account as investment items. In determining the deductible amount of other interest items for purposes of AMTI, interest expense on debt incurred or continued in order to invest as a limited partner or as a stockholder in an S corporation, where the taxpayer does not participate in management, is considered an itemized deduction; income from such an investment is considered qualified investment income.

Deductions that are subject to limitations under the regular tax rules are also subject to limitations in determining AMTI. Accordingly, itemized deductions that may be carried to other years for purposes of the regular tax, such as excess investment interest or excess charitable contributions, may not be deducted in computing AMTI in the current year.

The deduction for a net operating loss takes on a new meaning under the AMT provisions. For purposes of AMTI, the net operating loss deduction computed for regular tax purposes (other than any amount that arose before 1983) is not an allowable deduction. Instead, a separate computation of the carryover amount must be made, based on the principles of AMTI. Thus, taxpayers generating net operating losses are required to make separate carryover calculations so preference items do not reduce AMTI in previous or subsequent years.

The Load

In tax shelter investments, the term *load* refers to those costs borne by the investor that represent compensation to someone else. These "soft costs," which do not result in the acquisition of "hard" assets from which income or gain ultimately may be realized, come in many forms — sales commissions, professional fees, management fees, etc. They may be paid to the general partner (as reimbursement for costs incurred on behalf of the venture or as compensation) or to outsiders.

All investments are loaded in one way or another and that is not inherently bad. To the tax shelter investor, however, the load borne by a shelter investment has particular significance, for two reasons. First, there is the question of reasonableness. There is not much uniformity in shelter loading and some investments are more heavily loaded than others. Load costs may also be imposed in various ways. Some costs are front-end costs, paid from the investor's initial investment; this reduces the amount that is actually invested in assets to which an investor can look for income and ultimate gain. Other costs recur over the life of the investment and reduce the cash flow from operations available to the investor. One of the first decisions an investor must make in assessing a shelter investment is whether these costs are reasonable. This may be a subjective process, but an investor can lend some objectivity to that decision by comparing the load with that charged on similar investments by other promoters. Such information can be compiled from actual offerings or may be gleaned from tax shelter publications.

The second reason for concern about loading is the status of those costs for tax purposes. Some costs may be deducted when incurred, others must be capitalized initially and recovered as tax deductions over subsequent periods, and some costs cannot be deducted at all. Since the timing of tax deductions affects the return on an investment, it is important that costs be recovered as soon as possible. Although a shelter offering normally contains a discussion of the tax status of the various load costs, an investor may wish to confirm their status with a tax adviser.

Syndication costs. Tax law specifically prohibits the deduction of syndication costs as an expense. Thus, the costs of issuing and marketing partnership interests are not allowed as deductions either to the partnership or to any partner. As a result, investors can derive no tax benefit from such costs until the venture is terminated, and then only in the form of a reduced gain or as a capital loss. Syndication costs generally include brokerage fees and sales commissions, securities registration fees, certain legal and accounting fees, costs for printing the prospectus or offering memorandum, and other selling expenses. The total of these costs usually is significant.

Organization costs. Like any business, a tax shelter partnership must incur certain costs in getting organized, such as legal, accounting and filing fees. Although such costs may not be expensed for tax purposes as they are incurred, they may, by election, be deducted over a 60-month period.

Start-up expenditures. A new business entity may incur certain costs that are identified for tax purposes as "start-up expenditures." These are considered to be capital costs and cannot be expensed as they are incurred. At the taxpayer's election, however, these costs may be recovered through amortization over a period of not less than 60 months.

Additional Tax Returns

A tax shelter may have operations in a state other than that of the investor's legal residence. Some tax shelter entities (oil and gas partnerships, for example) have operations in more than one state. If those states impose a state income tax, an investor may be required to file an income tax return in each of those states. Multiple filing of these returns on a continuing basis can be bothersome and expensive.

Purchases and Sales Involving Deferred Payments

Tax shelters have used deferred payment transactions to achieve several objectives. Mismatching existed when accrual-method borrowers deferred payments to cash-method lenders. The allocation of payments between principal and interest was distorted to achieve greater depreciation deductions and investment tax credits. Interest deductions were accelerated to periods prior to the time they would have been recognized had an economic interest formula been employed. For these reasons, legislation was enacted both to prescribe the allocation of payments between principal and interest and to mandate symmetrical treatment between buyer and seller in those transactions in which an adequate interest rate is not charged. These provisions are quite complex and can significantly alter the tax consequences of deferred payment transactions.

Prepaid Expenses

In the past, many tax shelters — including oil and gas, research and development, and farming — relied on the deduction of prepaid expenses. Provided the prepayment was for valid business purposes and was not a deposit, these expenses were generally deductible in the year when paid. Now, a tax shelter using the cash method of accounting is no longer permitted to deduct such amounts until "economic performance" has occurred and the amount is paid. Economic performance generally occurs when services are performed, property is provided, or the use of property occurs. For example, economic performance for research and experimental expenditures occurs when the research work is performed. A special rule permits deductions for prepayments if economic performance occurs within 90 days after the end of the taxable year in which prepayment is made.

Accrued Expenses

Tax shelters using the accrual method of accounting are also subject to new rules. Previously, taxpayers could deduct an expense in the year in which all the events had occurred that determined the fact of liability and the amount could be reasonably determined. Actual payment was unnecessary to establish the deduction. Many tax shelters were structured to take advantage of these provisions and were permitted substantial deductions long before payments were required. All accrual-method taxpayers are now subject to the economic performance requirements described above. In certain circumstances, interest income and expense can be imputed for accrued but unpaid liabilities for services or the use of property.

Tax Penalties

Every tax shelter investor should be aware of certain penalty provisions in the tax law. One provision imposes a penalty on a taxpayer who overstates the value of property. The penalty can be substantial, up to 30% of the amount by which a taxpayer's income tax is understated as a result of the overstatement of value. Moreover, the interest rate on the tax due from an overvaluation is 120% of the regular interest rate.

Another penalty provision deals with the aggressiveness of taxpayers in reporting transactions for tax purposes. If a taxpayer has an underpayment of tax that is attributable to a "substantial understatement of income tax," a 10% penalty is imposed on that underpayment. For this purpose, a substantial understatement is defined as 10% of the tax required to be shown on the return, and the amount of such understatement for individuals must be at least $5,000. The penalty will not be imposed, however, if the taxpayer has "substantial authority" for the position that caused the understatement, or if the "relevant facts" affecting the taxpayer's treatment of the item are "adequately disclosed" in the tax return.

Special exceptions to the substantial understatement penalty provisions apply to "tax shelter" situations. Disclosure alone is *not* sufficient to avoid the penalty in the case of any entity, plan or arrangement having tax avoidance or evasion as its principal purpose (a "tax shelter"). Further, the existence of substantial authority for such a "shelter" will avoid the penalty only if the taxpayer "reasonably believed" that such tax treatment was "more likely than not" the proper treatment.

The substantial understatement penalty may be waived upon showing that the taxpayer acted with reasonable cause and good faith. Further, this penalty is not imposed on items subject to the valuation overstatement penalty discussed previously.

Authoritative interpretations by regulations, rulings, and judicial decisions concerning the penalty provisions are still developing, so knowledgeable assessment of how they may affect tax shelter investors requires speculation and judgment. It seems reasonable to assume, however, that a penalty may be imposed for obvious abuse of tax rules, such as a flagrant overvaluation of assets to obtain tax benefits.

Registration With the Internal Revenue Service

Several reporting requirements apply to tax shelter partnerships and syndications. The promoter of a syndication must maintain a list of investors for scrutiny by the IRS. Tax shelter promoters are also required to register their promotions with the IRS and to identify the projected tax benefits. The shelter is subject to registration only if twice the tax *credits* plus all of the *deductions* from the shelter are projected to exceed twice the cash invested as of the end of any of the first five years of operation. However, IRS registration is not required unless the promotion is required to be registered with a federal or state securities agency (or is exempted from such registration) or the aggregate offering exceeds $250,000 and five or more investors are expected.

Partnerships in which there has been a transfer of a partnership interest during the year must report it to ensure that the ordinary income portion of the gain attributable to the transfer is properly reported by the transferring partner.

The Bona Fides of Tax Shelters

Although the good and the bad features of tax shelters must be considered by shelter investors, they are of little import when an investment lacks *bona fides*. Thus, a tax shelter investment transaction must be entered into in good faith by both promoters and investors — and certainly never with deceit or fraud.

This does not mean that such investments must be free of controversy concerning their tax results; honest differences of opinion between the government and taxpayers have long been a natural and accepted part of our tax system. Basic to the legitimacy of such controversy, however, is the principle that taxpayers should not expect to reap tax benefits from transactions that have neither economic substance nor an objective to earn a profit beyond their tax savings. To do so may well expose a taxpayer to the severe penalties discussed above.

Profit motive. The government has many weapons in its arsenal to combat the allowance of tax shelter losses. Some of those have been discussed previously — the at-risk rules, the requirement that partnership allocations have substantial economic effect, etc. — but the challenge to the existence of a true profit motive can be as devastating as any. If a transaction lacks such motive, then expenses, losses, or credits that arise from it are generally not allowable.

Specific tax provisions disallow most losses and deductions for activities not engaged in for profit (the so-called hobby loss provisions). Although those provisions provide for a *presumption* of profit motive when an activity yields a profit in two of five successive years (seven years for breeding, training, showing or racing of horses), the government may overcome that presumption.

Economic substance. Lack of economic substance can be fatal to specific transactions on which the success of a tax shelter investment hinges. This situation can exist, for example, when the potential for profit and the risk of loss are lacking, or nearly so. For example, an interest deduction can be disallowed on debt arising from the purchase of an asset when the price paid so greatly exceeds the value of the asset that the debt cannot be considered *bona fide*. That result also causes the loss of tax basis in the asset on which depreciation deductions depend.

Overvaluation of assets and other tax return positions lacking adequate support are real dangers that must be avoided by shelter investors, not only because the anticipated tax benefits may be lost, but also (and perhaps more importantly) because of the substantial penalties to which the investor may be exposed (see page 28).

Accounting for the facts. The Internal Revenue Service has broad powers for challenging the way a taxpayer accounts for an investment or a transaction. For example, in order to "clearly reflect income," the IRS can require that an entity report income and expense transactions when they are earned (income) or incurred (expenses) rather than when they are received or paid. And the IRS can insist that the substance of a transaction be given effect rather than its mere form. For instance, when a loan to a partnership evidenced by a note has enough characteristics of a risk investment (equity capital), it may be treated as such rather than as a loan.

Radically different results of investment activities or transactions can flow from such government challenges if the attack is successful, with tax results detrimental to the investors. The lesson for investors is to be aware of the potential problems, read carefully the offering material that discusses those risks, and obtain competent tax advice.

Abusive shelters. Much has been said in recent years about abusive tax shelters, those that abuse the tax laws on which they are based (and ultimately, perhaps, the investor as well). A Treasury official has described such shelters in this way:

> An "abusive tax shelter" is a transaction without any economic purpose other than the generation of tax benefits that typically employs exaggerated valuations of assets and otherwise mischaracterizes critical aspects of the transaction.

The Internal Revenue Service informally makes the following distinction between tax shelters that are abusive and those that are not:

☐ Abusive tax shelters involve transactions with little or no economic reality, inflated appraisals, unrealistic allocations, etc., where the claimed tax benefits are disproportionate to the economic benefits. Such shelters typically seek to evade taxes.

☐ Non-abusive tax shelters involve transactions with legitimate economic reality, where the economic benefits outweigh the tax benefits. Such shelters seek to defer or minimize taxes.

Although those definitions may not be perfect, they will suffice. An investor who encounters an investment opportunity that *appears* to fit the definition of an abusive shelter would do well to shun it. Otherwise, the investor may be faced with substantial penalties as well as loss of the hoped-for tax savings.

The Quiet Shelters

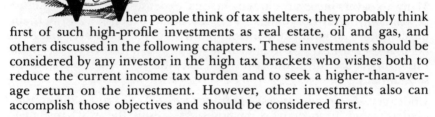

When people think of tax shelters, they probably think first of such high-profile investments as real estate, oil and gas, and others discussed in the following chapters. These investments should be considered by any investor in the high tax brackets who wishes both to reduce the current income tax burden and to seek a higher-than-average return on the investment. However, other investments also can accomplish those objectives and should be considered first.

Some investments are truly tax shelters but generally are not thought of as such, perhaps because they are so obvious. Yet they can create deductions that defer taxes for considerable periods, can shift income among family members to permanently reduce overall family tax burdens, and can shield current income from immediate taxation. The more effective of these investments and income-shifting transactions include:

☐ The "asset value freeze" technique.

☐ The short-term trust.

☐ The spousal remainder trust.

☐ The sale and leaseback of business property between family members.

☐ The Keogh (or H.R.10) plan.

☐ The individual retirement account (IRA).

☐ Cash value life insurance.

☐ Deferred annuities.

The Asset Value Freeze Technique

"Asset value freeze" techniques have been developed to minimize the overall income and estate tax burdens of family members who possess substantial holdings of such assets as closely held businesses or other major investments. Basically, these techniques seek to "freeze" at their current values the holdings of older family members and to divert to younger family members future increases in the value of assets or a business.

Although these techniques seek primarily to minimize estate taxes, they may also include features that minimize overall family income tax burdens. Their technical complexities preclude a full discussion of such plans here. Investors who believe that such a plan would be appropriate to their own family's overall financial situation should seek expert legal and tax advice to determine whether these techniques are practicable and how they may be implemented in their particular circumstances.

The Short-Term Trust

Trusts are complex entities under tax law. Perhaps for that reason, many taxpayers fail to use them when they could serve a very useful purpose. When properly structured and properly used, however, the complexities of trusts are overshadowed by their favorable results.

Many taxpayers incur substantial personal expenses that ordinarily must be paid with after-tax dollars. This can be an expensive and perhaps burdensome commitment. For example, a taxpayer in the 50% marginal tax bracket must earn $100 of income to pay $50 of such expenses. With the proper use of a short-term trust, this cost can be reduced substantially.

Under certain circumstances, a grantor (creator) of a trust is not considered its owner for income tax purposes. As a result, the trust's income is not taxed to the grantor during the trust term. The burden of current income taxes is shifted to the designated income beneficiary (if it is distributed currently) or to the trust itself (if the income is accumulated for future distribution).

The effectiveness of a short-term trust as a tax shelter device is measured by how well it shifts taxable income from a high-bracket taxpayer to a low-bracket taxpayer. Such income shifting can achieve significant tax savings. In some cases, the low-bracket beneficiary may pay no taxes at all on the trust income. Short-term trusts are particularly useful in situations where a grantor must accumulate funds for a minor child's education or provide support for an aged relative. They may not be used, however, to discharge a legal support obligation of the grantor, as determined by local law. (In some states, providing a college education may be a legal support obligation.)

The use of short-term trusts requires consideration of many factors, such as the type of property used to fund the trust, availability of gift tax exclusions, distributions or accumulations of income, etc. A taxpayer should therefore seek competent legal and tax advice before establishing such trusts.

The Spousal Remainder Trust

Since the law has removed virtually any significant family tax savings through the use of below-market-rate loans, taxpayers may want to consider the spousal remainder trust as an alternative income-shifting technique. If properly drafted and administered, these trusts can shift income to a family member for a desired length of time, while avoiding gift taxation through the use of annual exclusions and the gift tax marital deduction.

As with the short-term trust, the income interest of the spousal remainder trust is given to a lower-bracket taxpayer. However, the trust principal passes to the grantor's spouse upon termination of the trust rather than reverting to the grantor.

In addition to the income tax savings, the grantor of a spousal remainder trust does not incur any estate tax liability since the grantor does not retain a reversionary interest; therefore, no trust contributions need to be included in the grantor's gross estate. Thus, the spousal remainder trust can serve as a vehicle for shifting assets to the spouse with the smaller estate.

Similar to short-term trusts, trust income that is used to discharge the grantor's legal obligations is taxable to the grantor.

While the spousal remainder trust is not a new concept, it has not been widely used. Accordingly, a taxpayer should obtain competent legal and tax advice before establishing such a trust. However, the spousal remainder trust's flexibility, its significant income shifting potential and estate planning compatibility warrant close consideration as an alternative to the short-term trust.

Sale and Leaseback of Business Property

A short-term trust may also be used to reap substantial family financial benefits through sale of business property by one member (generally a parent) to a trust whose income beneficiary is another family member (generally a child of the grantor). The trust then leases the property back to the seller, who obtains a business deduction for the lease payments against income taxable at high rates. Because the trust (or its income beneficiary) is in a low tax bracket, significant overall family tax savings may be realized.

Although some courts have sanctioned this type of arrangement, it has not fared as well in others. Accordingly, a taxpayer who contemplates such an arrangement should first seek expert legal and tax advice.

The Keogh Plan

The Keogh plan (also known as an H.R.10 plan) may be one of the most attractive tax shelters today. It allows a self-employed individual (either a sole proprietor or a partner) to contribute annually a limited amount of income to fund retirement. The amount of the deductible contribution to a Keogh plan depends on the type of plan. In the case of a defined-contribution plan, the deduction is limited to the lesser of $30,000 or 15% of self-employment income; for a money-purchase plan, the limitation is the lesser of $30,000 or 20% of self-employment income. A defined-benefit plan, on the other hand, may yield a deduction as high as 100% of self-employment income. Because the contribution is currently deductible and the income on the accumulated contributions compounds free of current taxes desirable investments for such funds would be safe, high-income assets, not assets that produce tax deductions or credits.

Establishing a Keogh plan can involve many factors, such as the necessity for covering employees and restrictions on withdrawals. Accordingly, such a plan should not be undertaken without expert advice and assistance.

IRAs

Individual retirement accounts or IRAs are another means for obtaining current tax deductions for payments made to fund retirement and for sheltering retirement plan investment income from current taxation. In their results, IRAs are akin to Keogh plans; however, the allowable contribution amount that can be annually deducted for IRAs is considerably less—$2,000 ($2,250 if a nonworking spouse is also covered). Married taxpayers treat each spouse's earned income separately; each spouse may have an IRA account and deduct a maximum of $2,000. Beginning in 1985, alimony received is treated as compensation for purposes of determining the IRA limitation. Participants in Keogh plans may also establish an IRA, thus increasing their annual deductible contributions toward their retirement to as much as $32,000 where a defined-contribution or a money-purchase plan has been used ($32,250 if a nonworking spouse is also covered). Similar increases are obtainable where a defined-benefit plan has been established.

Unlike Keogh plans, IRA contributions may be based on an individual's salary and other earned income, regardless of whether it is self-employment income. IRAs can be used by individuals who also are covered by an employer's retirement plan.

Another use for an IRA is to roll over certain distributions from qualified retirement plans. This enables an individual to defer paying tax on the distribution while accumulating taxfree earnings.

Although IRAs are considerably less complex than are Keogh plans, they too should be implemented with professional guidance.

Cash Value Life Insurance

For many years, life insurance has been viewed as a socially desirable investment, and the tax law has provided significant tax benefits to owners and beneficiaries of permanent (whole life) insurance policies. Specifically:

☐ Policy death benefits are not taxable to policy beneficiaries even though they may substantially exceed the premium paid by the policyowner.

☐ No tax is imposed on policy cash value accumulations if the policy is held until death. Accumulated policy cash values can be borrowed without triggering a tax on the policy earnings.

☐ Policy loan interest paid is generally deductible if certain tax requirements are met.

In recent years, numerous new life insurance products have entered the marketplace. Competent advice should be obtained to assist in choosing the appropriate type of policy to meet the purchaser's specific needs.

Deferred Annuities

Deferred annuities provide investors with the opportunity to accumulate investment earnings on a tax-deferred basis. Contributions to deferred annuities are not deductible. However, earnings on the invested funds accumulate tax deferred until withdrawn by the policyholder. If taxpayers purchase a deferred annuity when their income is high, and withdraw funds systematically during retirement years when their taxable income is decreased, both a tax deferral and a reduction of total taxes can be obtained.

Several years ago, some deferred annuities were marketed as short-term investment vehicles. Recent tax legislation has reduced the desirability of deferred annuities for short-term investment needs, while at the same time confirming the favorable tax benefits afforded deferred annuities in their traditional role as favored long-term savings vehicles.

Chapter 4

Real Estate

nvestments in real estate are one of the most popular forms of tax shelter investment — and for good reasons. Real estate offers much that other forms of investment do not. One basic advantage it uniquely enjoys is that many investors have a natural affinity for it. It is tangible, visible, accessible. You can touch it, see it, walk on it. It is solid, secure, and will be here tomorrow as it is today.

These may be sound reasons for real estate's popularity, but there are better reasons why it has been and will continue to be one of the most sought-after means for achieving the goals of tax shelter investors.

Why Real Estate?

Historically, real estate has always been considered a good investment, prized by individuals and governments alike. A cynic might say that more wars have been fought for property than for principle. Whether that is true does not change the fact that investors have long favored real estate as an investment vehicle.

Many investors view real estate as the preferred way to achieve the goals of tax shelter investing. But before an investor commits to a real estate investment, the investor should have more than a *general feeling* about its desirability as an investment. The investor must focus on specifics, on the reasons why real estate is a preferred investment. Even if some of those reasons are intangible, theoretical or subjective, they all must be considered and measured against the goals of tax shelter investing.

Tradition

It is commonly accepted that real estate has *traditionally* been a good investment. Most people seem to believe that implicitly. Because of that belief, real estate probably has a decided advantage over other investments in the spirited competition for the tax shelter dollar. However, an investor must realize that tradition, although demanding respect, is basically a handing down of beliefs or a continuity of attitudes; it is not a sure measure of investment quality. Every investment must be judged on its own unique facts, and in real estate (along with tests common to all tax shelter investments) that means location, population, demographics, traffic, occupancy, comparable values, overall economic conditions, and a host of other factors that may affect the economic viability of the investment.

Leverage

Real estate offers the advantage of leverage, which is a magnification or multiplication of purchasing power. Leverage is a fulcrum that can move and close a $1,000,000 real estate transaction with the investment of perhaps $250,000 or less. It is the ability to partially finance a property acquisition with someone else's money.

The value of leverage can be readily appreciated by noting that property appreciation generally accrues wholly (but not always, as discussed later) to the benefit of the owner of the property, while the lender's rewards are fixed. Assume, for example, that a property with a total cost of $1,000,000, $250,000 of which is equity and $750,000 of which is debt, increases in value to $1,200,000. That 20% increase in value accrues fully to the equity owner (an increase of 80%); the lender's position remains unchanged.

Hedging Against Inflation

Hedging is a defensive move to protect against the possibility of loss. One of the most common forms of financial loss in our economy is the effect of inflation on purchasing power. A good investment cannot stand still in terms of the dollars it commands as the measure of its value. Its value in dollars must move in concert with the movement in the price of goods and services. If an investment responds in that way, it is considered a good hedge against inflation. Real estate generally has done that, and that is one of the very good reasons for its popularity as an investment.

Appreciation

In the world of investments, appreciation is not a social grace; it is a word that describes an increase in value. To achieve a *real* increase in value, however, an investment's appreciation must exceed the increase in value due to inflation. Real estate has been known to achieve that, but not with certainty; like any other investment, the value of real estate can also decline. Whether a real estate investment accomplishes the appreciation goal set by an investor depends on future events, economic conditions, etc. Although none of these can be known at the time of investment, they can be anticipated. That is part of the process of evaluating risk and reward, a process that is discussed later.

Limited Liability

Every investor would like to limit personal liability for an investment to the amount invested. If the investment turns sour, the investor can take the loss and put it out of mind. But some investments don't allow an investor to do that — investing in stock on margin, for example. In other cases, an investor may be able to limit personal liability, but at the cost of limiting the tax benefits as well.

With real estate investments, an investor can have the best of both worlds, limiting personal liability without limiting the tax benefits. This is possible through use of the limited partnership form of organization previously discussed and through the use of nonrecourse mortgage loans for which the investor is not personally liable. Unlike the result in other tax shelter investments, this immunity from personal liability to mortgagees does not limit the tax losses of real estate investors.

Marshaling Investment Power

It is often desirable for a group of small investors to pool their resources to acquire a significant real estate investment that none could have afforded alone. This marshaling of the investing power of a number of investors affords a greater opportunity for them to participate in prime real estate projects. It also gives those investors access to experienced real estate managers whose expertise otherwise would be unavailable. An investor must realize, however, that this method of investing constitutes buying "at retail"; an investor who is financially able to carry the same investment property alone might be able to do so at less cost.

Spreading the Risk

Real estate offers an investor an opportunity to spread investment risk. For example, an investor who has $100,000 to invest in real estate need not put it all at the risk of one real estate development. A cautious investor may prefer to spread the risk over two or more investment properties. Such an investor also may wish to spread the risk among different real estate promoters or managers.

Building Equity

An investor's equity position in an investment can be increased through inflation and appreciation. It also can be increased through debt reduction. As an investor's equity position increases, so does the investor's ability to leverage the investment. That increased leverage may be used to provide additional funds through refinancing the original mortgage debt.

Cash Flow

It is possible that a real estate investment may not produce a positive cash flow (even with tax savings) during its start-up years, although many do. After that initial period, however, a good real estate investment should provide cash flow to its owners. What the owner does with that cash may ultimately contribute to the success of a tax shelter investor. For example, such cash can be invested for later use to cushion the harsh tax results of turnaround, either through payment of post-turnaround taxes or through additional shelter investments to shield post-turnaround income.

Why Not?

Although the advantages of real estate investments are impressive, real estate is not necessarily the answer to every tax shelter investor's prayers. Like any other investment, it has its downside, which must be considered.

The Value Judgment

The value judgment in a real estate transaction has nothing to do with moral discernment, but it may be no less difficult. It is simply a question of assessing value as measured by dollars. Is the investment worth the price that has been assigned to it? So many factors bear on the value of real estate that an investor may be hard-pressed to consider them all. Yet the question must be answered, if necessary with the assistance of an investment adviser.

Marketability / Liquidity

An investor in real estate (and particularly one who has invested through a partnership) must accept the fact that such an investment typically entails a long-term commitment, since real estate normally cannot be sold quickly. The amount of time and effort required to sell real estate depends on many factors, including price, demand, economic conditions, availability of financing, interest rates, and others. If an investor's real estate position is represented by a partnership interest, it may be even more difficult to convert the investment into cash or other property. Thus, an investor who must be able to move out of investments quickly may find that a real estate investment does not suit such needs.

Reverse Leverage

An investor who takes advantage of leverage in buying real estate must realize that when selling the property, its purchaser probably will be seeking the same thing. Thus, the investor may have to accept installment receivables as part of the sales consideration. An investor in real estate should be prepared to accept the seeming irony of this "reverse leverage" potential of such investments, particularly when traditional real estate financing is scarce and expensive.

The term "reverse leverage" may also describe what happens to an investor when the value of property declines. In the example on page 37, assume that the value of the property *decreases* 20%. In that case, the $200,000 decrease affects only the owner's equity, which decreases 80%; the lender's position is unimpaired.

Size of Investment

The amount of cash invested in a real estate venture can be leveraged into a much larger investment, as discussed earlier. This does not necessarily mean, however, that the initial cash requirement is a modest one.

Most real estate projects assembled by tax shelter promoters are substantial and they require significant front-end cash investments. An investor who seeks real estate as an investment must be willing to make that commitment to achieve tax shelter objectives.

Additional Investment

An investor in real estate through a limited partnership ordinarily commits to an investment of a specified amount. But as a practical matter, an investor should understand that circumstances ultimately may require an additional investment. If a real estate venture encounters unanticipated cash flow problems, investors may be forced to choose between investing additional funds to keep the venture afloat or letting the lender foreclose. The first alternative may be forced on investors to avoid the undesirable tax consequences of the second. The general partner sometimes may agree to fund certain deficits through loans to the partnership. An investor should determine whether the general partner has agreed to do so before investing.

Financing the Investment

In the past, the maximum cost of financing a real estate investment was known, since suppliers of permanent financing (banks, savings and loans, insurance companies, pension funds, etc.) generally were willing to provide capital on a fixed-rate, long-term basis. It was a definite advantage to have that certainty of financing costs, but an investor in real estate today may have to settle for less. As a consequence of the volatility of interest rates in recent years, many lenders now are unwilling to provide funds under the inflexible conditions of the past. Lenders may want the right to adjust interest rates during the term of the loan, perhaps through renegotiation at some predetermined time or through relatively early maturity of a "balloon payment." If the resulting cash requirements cannot be met from funds provided by the property's operations or from refinancing, the investors may be the only source for the required funds.

A Piece of the Action

At one time, mortgage lenders were willing to limit their reward for participating in real estate ventures to the interest earned on the loan. That practice is fast-changing. A lender today may demand "a piece of the action" as an inducement to make a loan. This might be represented by participation in a property's rental income or in the proceeds from its sale. The lender also may take an equity position in the property, similar to the other investors. Although the lender's equity position would command a part of the tax benefits that otherwise would have gone to the investors, what is more important is whether the lender is actually putting up money for the equity position or whether the other investors are "carrying" the lender through their own investments.

An investor should be aware that the distinction between debt and equity is not always clear-cut under tax rules. A financing arrangement that is considered debt by a lender may be interpreted as an equity investment by the tax law. Should that happen, the tax benefits otherwise available only to the investors must be shared also with the lender.

Form of Investment

A real estate investment need not take the form of a limited partnership. Such investment can be made through various forms — solely by one individual, through participation in a general partnership, through a trust, indirectly by investment in the shares of a corporation that actually makes the real estate investment, through a real estate investment trust, etc. But no form of ownership is better suited to the needs of the tax shelter investor than the limited partnership. Some of the reasons for this have already been discussed, such as limited liability. Other reasons are discussed below.

Tax Considerations

Most of the tax advantages and disadvantages associated with real estate investments were discussed generally in Chapter 2. It would be helpful, however, to look more closely at those items that are most important to real estate investments and some others that are peculiar to real estate.

At-Risk Limitations

As was noted earlier, the at-risk rules limit substantially the depreciation and investment credit benefits available through most tax shelter investments. Although this also is true of investment credits (not rehabilitation credits) available through a real estate partnership, investment credits are not usually a significant element in real estate ventures. The tax attribute critical to all real estate investments (except those involving raw land) is depreciation. Fortunately, real estate losses are not subject to the constraints of the at-risk rules; depreciation is allowed in full without regard to an investor's personal liability for encumbrances on depreciable real property.

Depreciation

The depreciation deduction is real estate's great strength — its cornerstone — as a tax shelter investment. It is a tax-deductible, noncash charge against income; its tax benefits can be used to partly finance the various costs of owning real estate, including the nondeductible cost of debt reduction.

Most depreciable property placed in service after 1980 is subject to the Accelerated Cost Recovery System (ACRS) depreciation rules. Although the ACRS rules fall short of perfection, they are a vast improvement over the previous systems, since ACRS eliminates any grounds for controversy over useful lives, salvage values, etc. Taxpayers need no longer live in fear that an asset to which they had assigned a useful life of say 20 years or so, will be found by the Internal Revenue Service to possess the endurance capacity of the ancient pyramids.

Under ACRS, depreciable assets are neatly compartmentalized into five property classes for which costs may be recovered over 3, 5, 10, 15, and 18 years. The real estate investor is most concerned with the 18-year property class.

18-year property. Most real estate placed in service after March 15, 1984, including elevators and escalators, falls within the ACRS 18-year property class. This means that the cost of such property is recoverable through depreciation over an 18-year period. (Note: A 15-year recovery period applied to pre-March 16, 1984 additions that qualify for ACRS.) Annual depreciation is determined by reference to a table (see Appendix B) that uses an accelerated 175% declining-balance method of depreciation, switching to the straight-line depreciation method at the optimum point. The ACRS rules treat commercial and residential real estate the same and do not distinguish between new and used real estate; all are depreciated under the same recovery table.

Some exceptions. Certain real estate does not fit into the 18-year, 175% declining-balance depreciation class. The cost of low-income residential property is recoverable over 15 years, using a 200% declining-balance rate and switching to straight-line depreciation at the appropriate time. (Appendix C provides the recovery table that must be used for low-income housing.)

Another exception to the general real estate cost recovery rule is the recovery of costs incurred in rehabilitating low-income housing that the owner has elected to amortize over 60 months. Also excepted is the cost of leasehold improvements where the remaining lease term, including renewal options, is less than 18 years; the cost of those improvements is recoverable over the lease term.

Alternatives. The owner of real estate is not *required* to take advantage of the accelerated depreciation allowances provided by the ACRS tables for the 18-year property class. If it is advantageous to do so, a taxpayer may elect to recover the cost under the straight-line method of depreciation over 18, 35 or 45 years. This election is flexible in its application and can be made on a property-by-property basis. It must be made on the tax return for the year in which the property is placed in service and is irrevocable.

Why straight-line? On its face, the option to use straight-line depreciation in lieu of the accelerated method afforded by the ACRS rules seems something less than desirable. But that is not necessarily so, for the straight-line election allows the owner of real estate to thwart those nemeses of the tax shelter investor: depreciation recapture and tax preference deductions.

Depreciation recapture and its tax consequences were discussed on page 19. As previously noted, depreciation of nonresidential real estate under the 18-year accelerated recovery allowed by ACRS must be recaptured as ordinary income upon disposition of the property. The extent of that recapture depends on the gain realized and cannot exceed that amount.

Disposition of residential real estate depreciated under the ACRS 18-year property class also may result in depreciation recapture, but only to the extent that the accelerated depreciation exceeds the deduction that would have been allowed under the straight-line method.

The use of straight-line depreciation rather than accelerated cost recovery under ACRS avoids the need for recapture upon the disposition of real estate, both residential and nonresidential. Thus, the full gain realized is afforded favorable capital gain treatment.

In addition, straight-line depreciation may be advantageous if the property is sold in an installment sale. (See page 20 for a discussion of depreciation recapture on installment sales.)

It generally is preferable to use accelerated rather than straight-line depreciation for residential real estate, since the immediate tax savings from the accelerated deductions offsets the potential disadvantage of the limited depreciation recapture that may eventually result from disposition of the property.

Whether an owner of nonresidential real estate should forgo the certainty of accelerated depreciation in favor of potential capital gain depends on a variety of factors, all open to question when the straight-line election must be made. These factors include the taxpayer's current and future tax brackets, the time value of money, the probable holding period and sale price of the property, and the basic issue of whether the property will be sold at all.

Obviously, whether or not to use straight-line depreciation is a decision that cannot be made with any certainty. But few decisions are clear-cut, particularly in taxation, where little is certain except change. The fluidity of our tax rules makes planning no less useful; thus, the owner of nonresidential real estate must assess the relative benefits of accelerated versus straight-line depreciation before reasonably accepting or rejecting the straight-line option. This assessment must be based on each taxpayer's unique facts. Appendix D, for example, shows one method that might be used by a taxpayer to make a reasoned decision. Based on the assumptions used there, the taxpayer should use accelerated cost recovery only if planning to hold the property for more than 25 years; otherwise, the taxpayer should elect straight-line depreciation.

The election to use straight-line depreciation for a real estate investment also rids a property owner of a potential tax preference item on which the alternative minimum tax may be imposed (see page 23). This result also must be considered in making accelerated versus straight-line depreciation decisions.

The decision may not be yours. One characteristic of a partnership is that most tax elections must be made by the partnership itself and not by the individual partners. Thus, an investor who owns real estate indirectly through investment in a partnership cannot personally elect to use straight-line depreciation in lieu of accelerated depreciation under ACRS. The general partner must make that decision, presumably basing it on the principle of the greatest common good. Unfortunately, that course may not yield the results that would be best for a particular partner's personal tax position. If possible, an investor should determine prior to investing in a real estate partnership whether the various tax elections will be exercised in a way that yields the best results for personal tax circumstances.

Investment Credit

The investment credit is available principally for investment in personal property (and certain other property not generally pertinent to real estate shelter investments); it ordinarily is not a primary consideration in a real estate investment. Certain costs incurred in the construction or purchase of *nonresidential* real estate, however, may qualify for the credit. These include the cost of drapes, carpets, movable partitions, special lighting, and exterior ornamentation. When such items are used property, however, the availability of the credit is limited. Elevators and escalators may also qualify for the credit, but only if their original use is by the taxpayer claiming the credit. The availability of such credits affects the economics of a tax shelter investment and must be considered in evaluating the shelter. One crucial consideration is the property's status under the leasing rules that deny the credit to noncorporate lessors except under prescribed circumstances (see Chapter 6). In such cases, proper planning is mandatory if the credit is to be secured.

Rehabilitation Credit

The rehabilitation credit is the means Congress has chosen to encourage restoration of older buildings. The credit is indeed a persuasive incentive to investors to return such structures to full productive use. The credit is based on the actual cost of rehabilitation and varies according to the type and age of the structure, as follows:

Type of Property	Required Age	Credit
Commercial structures	At least 30 years	15%
Commercial structures	At least 40 years	20%
Commercial or residential certified historic structures	—	25%

As is usual for obtaining tax benefits, rehabilitation costs must also meet certain specific requirements to qualify for credit:

☐ The rehabilitation must be substantial, which means that the costs incurred over a two-year period must exceed the greater of the structure's tax basis or $5,000.

☐ The costs on which the credit is claimed must be capital costs (not costs that are actually expenses, such as repairs) incurred after December 31, 1981.

☐ The costs must have a recovery period of 18 years (without regard to the actual economic useful life).

☐ At least 75% of the external walls of the rehabilitated structure must remain in place as external walls.

However, the law provides an alternative to the last requirement above, as follows:

☐ At least 50% of the external walls remain in place as external walls,

☐ At least 75% of the external walls remain in place as either external walls or internal walls, and

☐ At least 75% of the internal structure remains in place.

As was noted earlier, the rehabilitation credit incentive exacts a cost from those who use it. The taxpayer who earns the credit must reduce the basis of the property otherwise recoverable through depreciation by the amount of the credit. (This requirement is moderated for rehabilitation of certified historic structures, the basis of which must be reduced by only one-half the credit.) Should it later be necessary to recapture the credit (see the discussion below), the amount recaptured is restored to the tax basis of the property.

Availability of the rehabilitation credit also precludes the use of an accelerated depreciation rate; cost recovery is allowed only under the straight-line method. This requirement applies also to certified historic structures.

Recapture. The rehabilitation tax credit is subject to recapture by the taxpayer who earned it. This recapture is required if the credit property is disposed of within five years after the property was placed in service, as follows:

Year of Disposition	Percentage of Credit Recaptured
Within one full year after property is placed in service	100
Second year	80
Third year	60
Fourth year	40
Fifth year	20

Certified historic structures. To qualify for the credit available for restoration of certified historic structures, the rehabilitated structure must meet certain requirements. Generally, the structure must be one that is used in a trade or business or held for the production of income, and that is either listed in the National Register of Historic Places or located in a registered historic district and certified by the Secretary of the Interior to be of significance to the district. The rehabilitation expenditures must be certified by the Secretary as being consistent with the historic character of the property or the district in which the property is located.

Front-End Deductions

Like most shelter investments, real estate investments require the payment of certain costs at the "front end." Some of these costs are deductible at that time (so-called front-end deductions) and some are not. For example, syndication costs discussed previously (see page 26) are not deductible.

Certain other costs, common in real estate investment, provide no initial tax benefit. An investor should be aware of these and should question any investment that seems to contradict the following rules:

☐ Prepaid interest can be deducted only in the taxable year to which the interest applies.

☐ "Points" paid to secure a loan must be deducted ratably over the term of the loan.

☐ Interest and taxes paid or accrued during the construction period of real property must be capitalized and recovered over prescribed periods, the recovery period depending on the year the amounts were paid or accrued and the type of property (residential or nonresidential) on which they were incurred. (This rule does not, however, apply to low-income housing.)

Sometimes front-end deductions may be promised by way of accruing deductions for services provided by related partners that will not be paid until some time in the future. Again, the investor should be wary; deductions are generally only allowed as paid to a cash-basis related party.

Rental Payments

In the past, it was possible through a number of real estate investments to increase the tax benefits to the investors by having the cash-basis lessor agree to defer rents from the accrual-basis lessee (investor's partnership), sometimes until end of the lease term. The cash-basis lessor generally reported rental income in the year payment was received. The accrual-basis lessee claimed a deduction for rental expense in the year the all-events test was satisfied; that is, when the events fixing the liability had occurred and the amount could be determined with reasonable accuracy. Therefore, the lessee (investor) could claim an annual deduction during the term of the lease while the lessor deferred reporting income until the rent was actually received.

This result has been eliminated (generally effective for agreements entered into after June 8, 1984) for certain types of leases. The application of these rules depends on the terms of the lease, stated rental amounts, the existence of deferred or stepped rents, whether the lease is part of a sale/leaseback transaction and whether there is a tax-avoidance purpose. These rules do not apply to any lease involving total payments of $250,000 or less.

In general, income from any rental agreement where at least one payment allocable to the use of property during the calendar year will be paid after the close of the following calendar year, or any agreement that has "step rents," is required to be reported on the accrual method regardless of the parties' methods of accounting. Both the lessor and lessee are required to annually accrue the rent allocable to that period as specified in the lease agreement, even though the payment is deferred.

In addition, certain leases are subject to rules requiring rents to be "leveled." For any deferred or stepped rental agreement involving either a long-term lease or a sale/leaseback — or where tax avoidance is considered a principal purpose — rents and interest must be accrued based on the "constant-rental amount." This term refers to the amount that, if paid at the close of each lease period, would have a present value equal to the present value of the aggregate payments under the lease.

Flip-Flop

The opportunity for special allocations of tax attributes was previously identified as one of the advantages of the partnership form of organization. Like other features of tax shelter investments, however, that initial advantage ultimately may have its downside. In shelter parlance, this potential adversity is sometimes called "flip-flop." It identifies that time when special allocations have run their course and the sharing of partnership tax attributes shifts to reflect a new relationship between the general and the limited partners. This process usually involves a reallocation of profits between general and limited partners (for example, an allocation of 90% of taxable income/loss to limited partners may shift to an allocation of, say, 60%). This has particular significance to a real estate limited partnership that has used nonrecourse debt to finance its property acquisitions. In such case, the allocation of the nonrecourse debt to the partners for purposes of determining tax basis also shifts. Tax rules require that this reallocation of debt be treated as a cash distribution to those partners whose allocable portions of the debt were decreased. Although cash distributions from a partnership to its partners ordinarily have no tax consequences other than a reduction in the partners' tax basis in the partnership, a cash distribution that exceeds that tax basis results in the recognition of a taxable gain.

It is difficult to generalize about the potential detriment to an investor due to flip-flop reallocations, since the result depends on timing, the amount of debt reallocated, and the investor's tax basis in the partnership interest. Even so, an investor must consider flip-flop in assessing the desirability of a partnership investment and should plan for it before it actually occurs.

Exchanges

Sales or exchanges of property generally are events that require the recognition of gain or loss for tax purposes. There are exceptions to this general rule, however, and one of the most significant of those applies to exchanges of real estate. This exception covers certain exchanges of property held for productive use in a trade or business or for investment for other property of a "like kind." The exchange may consist of any combination of these properties and need not be business property for business property, or investment property for investment property; however, the properties must be of like kind. This requirement refers to the nature or character of the property and not to its quality or grade.

This like-kind exchange provision in the tax law affords significant opportunities for a taxpayer to exchange an equity position in one property for an equity position in another without recognizing the potential tax gain that would have been realized had the property been sold and the proceeds been reinvested in another property. By means of the exchange, the potential gain in the property disposed of can be reinvested in full without suffering diminution from income taxes. Thus, an investor who has a property with a tax basis of $100,000 and a fair market value of $300,000 can exchange that property for one with an equal fair market value without recognizing the gain of $200,000. This investor also could leverage the $300,000 of equity into a much larger investment, such as a $1,000,000 property encumbered by $700,000 of debt.

The nontaxability of like-kind exchanges results only in a *deferment* of gain recognition, not in its elimination. Thus, the potential gain in the first property is merely rolled over to the second and will be recognized if that property subsequently is disposed of in a taxable transaction. This rollover of gain is accomplished by requiring that the property received in the exchange take the same tax basis as the property relinquished in the exchange. In other words, tax basis in the property received must be forfeited to the extent of the unrecognized gain.

Like many areas of taxation, the like-kind exchange provisions can be rather complex. For example, like-kind exchanges can be complicated by the receipt of money or other property that does not qualify as like-kind property, by considerations of recapture of depreciation and investment credits, or by the relief from or assumption of debt. Furthermore, the property to be received must be identified within 45 days and the exchange must be completed within 180 days from the date the relinquished property is transferred. Therefore, such transactions must be carefully analyzed before they are entered into, although they generally are a major advantage in direct real estate ownership; the exchange of partnership interests, however, does not qualify for like-kind exchange treatment.

Involuntary Conversions

Real estate is sometimes lost through destruction or condemned by government authorities for a public use. In such case, the property owner's disposition of the property is an involuntary conversion. To require the taxpayer to pay taxes currently on a gain that is involuntarily realized (through insurance or condemnation proceeds) but reinvested in similar property would be inequitable. Accordingly, tax rules provide relief for a taxpayer under those circumstances. How much gain — all, part or none — must be recognized on a particular transaction depends on the extent to which the property owner receives property or reinvests in property that is "similar or related in service or use" to the property involuntarily converted.

The "similar or related in service or use" requirement of involuntary conversions may differ from the "like kind" requirements of tax-deferred exchanges. Although it has been the subject of considerable controversy between taxpayers and the government, some general rules can be stated with reasonable assurance. In doing so, it is necessary to distinguish between owners/users of property and owners/investors in property. It is also necessary to look to the circumstances under which property is involuntarily converted; that is, whether by condemnation or threat of condemnation or by destruction through fire, storm, etc. Thus, in cases of involuntary conversion through any event other than condemnation, an owner/user of property must reinvest in property having the same *end use* as the converted property, whereas owners/investors need only reinvest in property having the same *business purpose* as the converted property. In the case of a conversion of property through condemnation, the qualification of the replacement property is tested under the more liberal like-kind property rules of tax-deferred exchanges.

Although the rules governing the tax treatment of involuntary conversions are complex, such complexities do not detract from the advantages they offer an owner of real estate who suffers an involuntary conversion of the property.

Capital Gain

To realize a capital gain on the disposition of property is one of the most significant rewards that a tax shelter investment can offer. As noted in the discussion of the common attributes of shelter investments (Chapter 2), however, realization of long-term capital gain has become a more remote possibility because of the depreciation recapture rules. One of the great strengths of real estate as an investment is that it still offers a reasonable possibility for capital gain realization in spite of those recapture rules.

The capital gain potential of real estate arises from two sources. First, there is the actual appreciation in value that a real estate investment may enjoy (see page 37). Second, there is the limited depreciation recapture to which residential real estate is subject and the total elimination of depreciation recapture through use of straight-line depreciation (see page 42).

Types of Real Estate Investment

There are many types of real estate investment. A tax shelter investor may feel more comfortable investing in one type than in another. Real estate investments differ in many ways, including the extent of tax benefits available, the degree of risk exposure, the potential for capital gain, location, use, etc. Broadly speaking, however, real estate investments are either unimproved real estate or improved real estate. Although the discussion in this chapter is concerned principally with improved real estate, both types warrant consideration by a real estate investor.

Unimproved Real Estate

Unimproved real estate offers fewer of the attributes generally sought in a tax shelter than does improved real estate. One of the attributes that is missing is the availability of depreciation through which a noncash loss may be generated; simply stated, land may not be depreciated. That does not mean, however, that unimproved real estate is necessarily less desirable as a pure investment (tax shelter considerations aside), since it may offer as much potential for ultimate realization of long-term capital gain as does an investment in improved real estate.

Unimproved real estate is said to pass generally through three cycles before it is finally developed to its full potential. An investor may acquire it in any one of these phases, and the timing of the acquisition may bear heavily on the financial results of the investment.

The first phase, in which the property is wholly undeveloped, is that period (which may be protracted) when the property offers little potential for development opportunities in the foreseeable future. During this cycle, the land may be a poor investment from a cash flow standpoint because substantial carrying costs such as taxes and interest may be incurred before the property can be developed or sold at a gain.

In the second or predevelopment phase, the property is yet undeveloped but shows signs of potential for development in the reasonably near future. The value of the property begins to rise as a result of changes in general economic conditions, demographics, proximity of developments such as new highways, freeways, airports, manufacturing or commercial facilities, etc. It is during this period that the potential for gain may be greatest.

In its third and final phase, the development phase, the property still offers significant opportunities for gain, particularly to its developers. It also offers opportunities for long-term investors in improved property, such as tax shelter investors.

It is generally believed that an investment in unimproved real estate is ideally made as the second phase is beginning and is sold as the third phase begins. Unfortunately, these phases are not normally so clearly delineated as to ensure that investment can be made at the optimum time. Achieving the proper timing may depend on a degree of astuteness and expertise in real estate matters that is not usually possessed by tax shelter investors. Accordingly, the success of such investments may be wholly dependent on the knowledge and advice of others (and perhaps on a little luck) in selecting the right unimproved real estate property.

Current trends. A potential investor in raw land must understand that any generalities about the appropriateness of unimproved real estate as an investment can be only that — generalities. An investor must look to more specific factors that may bear on the ultimate success of the investment. One such factor is the recent trend among local governments of examining the economic question of whether additional tax revenues generated from the extension of their boundaries to encompass new developments will adequately cover the additional costs of municipal services that such expansion requires. Other trends, such as the movement to renovate older buildings (encouraged by special tax benefits) rather than to build new ones, also must be considered.

Improved Real Estate

Investment opportunities in improved real estate are so many and varied as to defy enumeration. Such investments may be urban or suburban, residential or commercial, high-rise or low-rise, new or used. They may take the form of office buildings, apartment buildings, shopping centers, hotels, warehouses, and other structures. They may be leased to tenants on a long-term basis or on a short-term basis; they may be leased to one tenant or to many; the lease rental may be fixed over the term of the lease or may be subject to escalation. This wide variety of selection is an advantage to an investor, however, since it allows considerable latitude in selecting the investment best suited to individual circumstances.

Improved real estate may be the investment that offers the greatest potential to the greatest number of tax shelter investors, since it is available in so many forms and provides most of the attributes (except, generally, the investment credit on personal property) that investors seek in a shelter investment.

Measuring Risk and Return

The desirability of a real estate investment can be determined only by assessing its risks and the projected return. This cannot be done with exactitude, since it involves intangibles in assessing risk and imponderables in computing the return on investment. This does not mean, however, that a reasonable assessment of a real estate tax shelter's desirability as an investment cannot be made.

Risk

How is risk measured? Many of the factors that enter into the risk evaluation of any tax shelter were discussed in Chapter 1 (see page 7). Other factors, such as related-party transactions and conflicts of interest, were discussed previously (see page 15). In addition to those, other risks are involved in real estate investments that must be considered by an investor.

Property values. The principal tax attribute of an investment in improved real estate is the depreciation deduction, which accounts for much if not most of the early tax losses. The depreciation deduction depends, of course, on the tax basis of the property from which it arises. Tax basis in property generally is determined by its cost; in a real estate venture, that means what the partnership has paid others to construct or purchase the real estate. Most real estate investments include both buildings and land. It is necessary to determine the cost of each, since land is not depreciable. This normally is no problem when they are acquired separately; in a lump-sum acquisition of both, however, the cost must be reasonably allocated between the two property interests. Much depends on the acceptance of that cost as the basis for the depreciation deduction. Accordingly, it should be supported by an expert appraisal or other appropriate documentation.

Some mention was previously made of the possibility of related-party transactions in tax shelter investments (see page 15). In addition to the need for diligence noted there, an investor also should be aware that the government may challenge the depreciation deduction on assets acquired from parties who are considered to be related to the tax shelter partnership. The government has successfully done so in cases where the purchase price of real estate so greatly exceeded its reasonable value that the debt incurred to purchase the property was found to be not *bona fide*. Since this type of transaction lacks economic substance, depreciation and interest deductions cannot be sustained. A successful challenge also may result in penalties imposed on the investor under certain circumstances (see page 28).

Feasibility. Another factor that enters into the assessment of risk in a real estate investment is its feasibility. Anticipated operating results is one factor that weighs heavily on feasibility, and that is discussed separately (see page 53). Other considerations also affect the feasibility of a venture. For example, the reasonableness of a proposed shopping center must be measured against the findings of demographic studies, the proximity of other centers, access from and to major thoroughfares, the quality of the proposed anchor store, etc. All of this information should be available to the investor. Although conclusions concerning the feasibility of a proposed venture may be based ultimately on subjective judgments, such subjectivity can be reduced through access to objective, factual information.

Reward

Like the measurement of risk, the measurement of reward for a tax shelter investment is imprecise at best. Yet reward must be measured by anyone considering an investment in real estate. Some of the factors that enter into that measurement are known with some certainty (for example, the amortization period of the mortgage and the recovery period for depreciation purposes), but some are based on estimates (such as occupancy rates, lease terms, operating expenses and future values). Taken together, these knowns and unknowns constitute the projected results of operations for purposes of estimating taxable income or losses, cash flow, etc. These projections are, of course, essential to the evaluation of a tax shelter investment because they are the basis of the investor's conclusion concerning the return likely to be realized on the investment.

About projections. It is important that an investor realize that the estimated or projected results of a real estate project are only as good as the assumptions on which they are based. No one can expect those assumptions to yield precise predictions of ultimate operating results; as Casey Stengel once said, "Making predictions is difficult and especially when it involves the future." The assumptions on which projections are based, however, must make sense to the investor.

A tax shelter offering memorandum should contain various schedules that show computations of the projected results of operations over a period of years and should disclose the assumptions on which the computations are based. The computations themselves can be checked by the investor or by an adviser. It is the conclusions drawn from those computations and the assumptions on which they are based, however, that is of most concern to the investor. For example, a typical projection for an office building or an apartment building includes assumptions concerning beginning amounts and subsequent changes in:

☐ Rental rates.

☐ Vacancies.

☐ Operating expenses, including utilities, taxes and insurance.

☐ Maintenance and repairs expenses.

☐ Property improvements.

☐ Tax treatment of various items.

In deciding whether to participate in the proposed real estate venture, an investor must decide whether the assumptions used in preparing projections of the property's operating results make sense. If the investor is not qualified to make that judgment, the investor should enlist the aid of an adviser, preferably someone who is familiar with the proposed project and/or the community in which it is to be built. This "kicking the tires" of the proposed investment is a prudent action preliminary to the final step of making the financial calculations that show the investor what to expect in the way of return on the investment.

Return on investment. Determining the rate of return is critical to the analysis of any tax shelter investment. The nature of some shelter investments make it difficult to determine a rate of return, due to the uncertainty of future results. In oil and gas and in research and development ventures, for example, the initial results depend heavily on tax consequences that can be determined with reasonable accuracy. Future results, however, are difficult to predict, for they depend on the success of efforts to discover an asset with continuing value. Real estate (or at least improved real estate) is well suited to a return on investment analysis, since the factors that determine its future operating results can be reasonably well estimated.

Return on investment is discussed in greater detail in Chapter 12.

Oil and Gas

Perhaps no tax shelter investment is better known and less understood than investments in oil and gas properties. The industry itself has a certain glamour about it, attributable no doubt to stories of the swashbuckling, hell-for-leather wildcatters who strike untold riches just as they spend their last dollar to sink a hole that others would never consider drilling. It has a less appealing image, too, due to impressions caused by the continuing concerns about energy supplies and the volatile pump price of gasoline.

To many, exploration for oil and gas is synonymous with certain preferred tax deductions called intangible drilling costs (IDC) and depletion, each of which has different meanings to different people. To some noninvestors, these terms represent government beneficences bestowed gratuitously on the high-bracket taxpayer; to some investors, they represent the ultimate in tax deductions and are preferred above all others. These deductions may also represent a badge of sorts that identifies an oil and gas investor as a member of a select group of individualists willing to run the risks that are a part of that last frontier called wildcatting.

None of these views, of course, is entirely accurate.

The Oil and Gas Industry

To better understand what the oil and gas industry really is, an investor should consider its relative position in today's topsy-turvy world. Probably no problem confronting the United States today is more compelling than that of energy, and particularly energy that has its source in oil and natural gas. In spite of all our efforts, we have been unable to produce from domestic sources sufficient reserves of oil and gas to supply our domestic needs. Efforts to find alternative sources of energy have resulted either in failure to produce those sources economically or in serious controversy over their safety.

Our Dependence

Oil and natural gas have long been important sources of energy in this country. Their use as fuels to heat our homes and move our automobiles are so common that they were taken almost for granted until we were forcefully reminded by events beyond our control that it is dangerous to do so. Their other uses in plastics and other products are so pervasive, and yet so unobtrusive, that many people are unaware of them. Our failure to recognize crude oil products in their many refined and extracted forms serves to accentuate, rather than diminish, its importance in our daily existence.

Since Edwin Drake drilled his famous well near Titusville, Pennsylvania in 1859, more than 2.7 million wells have been drilled in search of oil and gas in the United States. In spite of that drilling activity, the United States today has only 5.1% of the world's estimated proved reserves of oil and only 6.2% of its estimated proved reserves of gas. Although great strides have been made in energy conservation during the past few years, the United States currently satisfies over one-fourth of its crude oil and refined products demand through imports.

As revealing as this information about reserves and imports may be, its significance can be fully appreciated only in the context of the role that oil and gas plays in our total energy use. Of our total estimated sources of energy in 1984, oil is expected to account for approximately 42% and natural gas 25% — a total of 67% — of our total energy needs.

Drilling Activity

The dangers inherent in our continuing dependency on foreign sources for a significant part of our energy needs have heightened the urgency of our search for domestic reserves of oil and gas. This urgency was reflected in the record drilling activity in 1982, when more than 88,000 wells were drilled; subsequent economic events have since caused a marked decrease in the number of wells drilled to 79,000 in 1983, and an estimated 75,000 in 1984.

Drilling activity in the United States normally provides a wide selection of opportunities for oil and gas shelter investors, since most of the drilling (an estimated 83% in 1984) is carried on by independent oil and gas operators, the main source of oil and gas tax shelter drilling programs.

Refining

The oil and gas tax shelter investor ordinarily has little to do with the refining stage of the industry. Yet that stage is the market for whatever reserves the investor may be fortunate enough to acquire through participation in the drilling stage and it must be considered if the industry as a whole is to be put into its proper perspective.

The principal activity of the major oil companies is petroleum refining and the marketing of refined products. These companies' impact on the nation's economy can reasonably be suggested by their standings among the country's leading industrial corporations. In the 1983 Fortune 500 compilation of the major industrial corporations, the top 15 companies included nine corporations deriving their income principally from petroleum refining. Those nine companies alone accounted for 19% of the sales, 19% of the assets, and 23% of the net income of the *total* Fortune 500 group.

Finding Oil and Gas

There is only one sure way to find oil and gas, and that is to drill a hole to see if it's actually there. There has never been a lack of enterprising souls to do just that, many times in the face of incredible odds. There is much more involved in finding oil and gas, however, than drilling holes. Perhaps the most important of those activities is the selection of the acreage on which to drill and the acquisition of the rights to do so.

Selection

Selecting where to drill for oil and gas is an involved undertaking that requires drawing on the expertise of various sciences in order to determine a likely spot for drilling. A discussion of that process is beyond the scope of this book and is best left to the experts. It is suffices to note that site selection is far from an exact science, as witnessed by the fact that of the 79,000 wells drilled in 1983 (only 15,000 of which were wildcat wells) 24,000 resulted in dry holes. Even a productive well does not guarantee ultimate success, since some wells may never produce reserves sufficient to recover their drilling costs.

Before drilling can be undertaken, an operator must acquire the *right* to drill. That process is one in which the oil and gas investor should be interested, for it ultimately determines the extent to which the investor pays for the costs of drilling and participates in the revenues derived from the sale of any oil and gas that is found.

The Mineral Interest

Property consists of two parts — its surface and the minerals that lie beneath the surface. Both these parts may be owned by the same owner, in which case they are together known as a *fee interest*. In some cases, the mineral interest may be severed from the surface interest; each interest may thereafter change hands independently of the other, the surface interest carrying with it the right to use the surface of the property and the mineral interest carrying with it the right to exploit the minerals beneath the surface. It is this mineral interest that provides opportunity to the oil and gas tax shelter investor.

Yet smaller pieces. A mineral interest in property seldom stays intact, for the original owner of the full mineral interest is seldom the one who exploits it through exploration and development. The reason for this is simple enough. Although ownership of a full mineral interest entitles its owner to the minerals produced from the property, it also carries with it the obligation to pay whatever costs are incurred in finding the minerals through drilling, lifting the minerals found to the surface, finding a buyer for the minerals, etc. Since few owners of a full mineral interest, particularly fee owners, can afford to undertake the very substantial cost and risk involved in exploiting the minerals, they turn to someone else for help.

It is at this point that the full mineral interest is broken into smaller parts. Even though the mineral owner cannot personally afford to exploit the minerals, the owner obviously is not willing to part with them *gratis*; accordingly, the owner leases the rights to the minerals to another. Under the terms of the lease, the rights to exploit the minerals are transferred to the lessee, with the mineral owner or lessor retaining the right to a specified fraction of the proceeds realized from the sale of the minerals. This retained interest is called a *royalty interest*. The lessee, whose interest in the minerals is called a *working interest*, must pay all costs incurred in exploiting the property and is entitled to that part of the proceeds realized from the sale of the minerals that remains after the royalty interest has been satisfied.

The original working interest owner or lessee need not personally undertake the development of the minerals. This owner or lessee may subsequently assign most of the rights and all of the obligations under the lease to another. In that transaction, a further nonoperating or passive interest is separated from the operating or working interest, which continues to carry the full burden of the cost of exploitation. That separated interest may take the form of a royalty interest (known as an *overriding royalty interest*) that, like the original royalty interest, shares in the gross income from the property without sharing in any of the costs incurred to produce that income. It may also take the form of a *net profits interest*, which entitles its owner to share in the net profits from the property that are realized by the working interest after the payment of the royalty interest and certain other defined costs. Another form that it may take is that of a *carried working interest*. Although the carried interest bears none of the costs of exploitation, it normally does not share in the income from the property until those costs have been recouped by that part of the working interest that paid them. At that time, the carried interest begins to function as a normal working interest.

The rights to exploit an oil and gas mineral interest may move from one party to another in several transactions before exploitation actually begins. In each transaction, however, the income rights of the party that ultimately pays the costs that must be incurred to exploit the minerals are further diminished. This is a critical point for consideration by the oil and gas investor and is discussed below in more detail.

Development

The exploration and development stages of the oil and gas story are its most exciting chapters, for it is here that fortunes may be gained or lost. People will no doubt always be fascinated by that great roll of the dice called wildcatting and few can be impervious to the sheer magnificence of a discovery such as the great East Texas Field that has yielded over 4.7 billion barrels of oil since 1930 and that yet has over 1.2 billion barrels in place. But that is the stuff of which dreams are made, an oil and gas investor needs to be more practical in viewing the possible results of the drilling stage of an investment.

The drilling of an oil or gas well is an expensive proposition. The cost of the well depends both on the depth of the hole and on the difficulty encountered in its drilling. From spudding to completion, a variety of costs are incurred for items with names that may seem strange to those unfamiliar with the industry — core-hole, deadman, logging, drill-stem, swabbing, fracturing, acidizing, "mud," surface casing, stabilizers, guideshoes, centralizers, "Christmas trees," treaters, separators, flow-lines, tank batteries, the list goes on and on. What is most important to the oil and gas investor, however, is the status of each of these items for tax purposes; that is, whether they are costs that can be deducted as expenses as they are incurred or whether they are costs that must be capitalized and recovered through depreciation or depletion.

In recognition of the risks involved in drilling for oil and gas, our tax laws allow certain costs — that otherwise would be classified as capital costs — to be deducted as current expenses. These costs are generally referred to as intangible drilling costs (IDC); their significance to an oil and gas investor is discussed later.

Oil and Gas as a Tax Shelter

Generally speaking, there is no question about the viability of oil and gas investments as a tax shelter. They offer some unique tax advantages that other types of shelter investments do not, such as the deductions for IDC and percentage depletion. When they are successful, they may yield a greater after-tax return than do other investments. On the other hand, oil and gas investments carry with them certain disadvantages, such as their high degree of risk. That risk is so great that an investment in an oil and gas exploratory drilling program may result in the total loss of the amount invested, a result not ordinarily found in other types of investments. Accordingly, an investment in oil and gas should be undertaken by an investor only after careful consideration of the many factors that bear on its suitability to individual tax and other circumstances.

The Advantages of Oil and Gas Investments

The advantages of oil and gas as a tax shelter investment are principally these:

☐ The deduction for intangible drilling costs (IDC).

☐ The deduction for percentage depletion.

☐ The investment tax credit.

☐ The potential for capital gain.

Two of these advantages (IDC and percentage depletion) are unique to oil and gas tax shelters; the others are attributes shared with a variety of other investments.

The IDC deduction. The deduction for intangible drilling and development costs is significant to an oil and gas investor for several reasons. First, such costs incurred on productive wells are costs that ordinarily would represent capital costs recoverable through depletion or depreciation; these costs, however, have been granted special status for tax purposes that allows them to be deducted as they are paid or incurred. Second, the intangible costs represented by the IDC deduction account for approximately 65%-70% of the total costs incurred to drill a productive well. IDC incurred on nonproductive wells generally are referred to as "dry hole costs." These costs also are deductible as paid or incurred. Thus, a significant portion of the amount invested in an oil and gas drilling program ordinarily is recovered through tax deductions at an early stage of the program, preferably in the year of investment.

A cash-basis taxpayer ordinarily can deduct expenses for tax purposes when they are paid; however, *prepayments* of expenses generally are not deductible except under certain narrow circumstances. An investor in oil and gas may, under certain prescribed conditions, currently deduct prepayments of IDC. This deductibility can be important to an investor, since such prepayments sometimes are necessary. The deduction for prepaid IDC requires that the payment from which it arises be "irretrievably out of pocket" and not merely a deposit that later may be returned. Payments under a turnkey drilling contract, for example, normally meet this requirement and their use is common.

The above restrictions have been tightened by adding additional requirements in order to secure a current deduction for a cash-basis "tax shelter." Rules effective after March 31, 1984, define a "tax shelter" to include many of the typical forms of oil and gas investments.

A cash-basis "tax shelter" may not deduct any item until it is paid *and* economic performance occurs. An exception is provided if economic performance occurs within 90 days after the close of the tax year. In the case of an oil and gas "tax shelter," economic performance occurs when the well is "spudded." The deduction under the 90-day exception is limited to a taxpayer's "cash basis" in the tax shelter, which specifically excludes most borrowings.

A traditional turnkey drilling contract referred to above is one that requires the driller to drill a well and, if commercial production is obtained, to equip the well to such stage that the operator may turn a valve and the oil will flow into a tank. It is a unique transaction, since it shifts the risks of drilling from the operator to the driller, who must drill to the contract depth for a fixed price, regardless of the time, materials or other expenses that are actually needed to drill the well. Although an operator may pay a significant premium for such a contract, there sometimes are business considerations that mandate such an arrangement.

The depletion deduction. The depletion deduction for which an oil and gas investor ordinarily will qualify is unique because it is a statutory concept ("solely a matter of legislative grace," as the Supreme Court has described it) that is not based on economic or geological concepts of depletion. The depletion concept recognizes that the production of oil and gas results in the exhaustion of a capital investment and our income tax laws generally do not impose a tax on capital. The depletion allowance is measured by applying a fixed percentage rate to the value of minerals produced and sold. Accordingly, it generally bears little relationship to the actual capital investment in the minerals and, over time, may exceed that amount.

Generally, the percentage depletion allowance for oil and gas was repealed in 1975; fortunately for investors, that repeal included various exceptions. One of those, the exception for independent producers and royalty owners (generally, those whose average daily production of oil and gas does not exceed 1,000 barrels), applies to most tax shelter investors in oil and gas. Under that exception, percentage depletion generally is allowed at a rate of 15% of gross income, limited in each case to 50% of the taxable income from the property (before the depletion deduction). There are other exceptions that may qualify certain gas production for a 22% depletion rate.

Investment tax credit. A successful oil and gas well requires the installation of a significant amount of equipment in order to produce and save the minerals. Depending on the type of drilling program in which investors participate, the investors may or may not bear the cost of that equipment. If they do, the investors are entitled to an investment credit of 10% of the cost of most property. The depreciable basis of equipment on which the full 10% credit is claimed must be reduced by one-half of such credit amount. Alternatively, an 8% credit can be claimed with no similar basis reduction.

Capital gain. The sale of a producing oil or gas property that results in a gain may result in income taxable at favorable long-term capital gain rates (a maximum rate of 20% for individuals). Whether such a result occurs, of course, depends on the value of the property's reserves. Even so, a part of the gain realized is classified as ordinary income due to certain recapture provisions discussed later (see page 61).

And the Disadvantages

Although tax shelter investments in oil and gas are favored by certain provisions of tax law, they also are subject to certain downside exposures that must be considered by an investor. Generally, these disadvantages include:

☐ High degree of risk.

☐ Recapture of certain tax benefits.

☐ Limitation on depletion deduction.

☐ Special taxes.

☐ At-risk requirements.

Some of these disadvantages are unique to oil and gas investments; some are not. Each is discussed below.

Risk. Risk of loss is not unique to oil and gas investments; the *high degree* of risk, however, is generally considered to be so.

Generally speaking, drilling for oil and gas *is* risky — a commonly quoted industry statistic is that only one of ten wildcat wells is successful — and an investor stands to lose all of the capital invested in a drilling venture. As a practical matter, however, most shelter investors do not participate only in the drilling of wildcat wells; some investors do not participate in that type of drilling at all. An investor can control the degree of risk to be assumed by several means. For example, the investor may limit the risk assumed by participating only in *development* drilling rather than *exploratory* drilling. (Types of drilling programs are discussed on page 67.) The investor may also limit such risk by splitting the total investment among different types of programs. Another possibility is for the investor to choose a program based on *where* drilling will be done, since some parts of the country offer more promising prospects for finding oil and gas than others.

Although the risk of drilling a dry hole should not be minimized, an investor should realize that all need not be risked on a single roll of the dice. Furthermore, an investor should realize that risk is not confined to the chance of drilling a dry hole. There are other risks, such as the reputation of the promoter and the extent to which the investment is being promoted, that may be equally important. Such risks are discussed later.

Recapture of tax benefits. Recapture of prior tax benefits, such as depreciation and investment credits, upon disposition of property is not unique to oil and gas investments. There is one recapture requirement, however, that is unique — the recapture of IDC.

As was noted above, the sale of a producing oil and gas property at a gain generally results in the realization of a *capital gain*, assuming holding-period requirements are satisfied. However, the IDC recapture requirements cause such gain to be recast, in whole or in part, as *ordinary income*. The extent of that ordinary income recognition is limited to the amount previously deducted as IDC, reduced by the amount by which the depletion deduction allowed on the property would have been increased had the deducted IDC been capitalized and recovered through cost depletion.

Limitation on depletion. Although percentage depletion is normally allowed to an oil and gas investor under the independent producer exemption discussed previously (see page 59), that deduction cannot be used currently without limitation. Current deduction of percentage depletion cannot exceed 65% of a taxpayer's taxable income, computed without regard to the percentage depletion allowance (and certain other adjustments). Any amount in excess of that limitation, however, can be carried forward and deducted in subsequent years, again subject to the 65% limitation.

Alternative minimum tax. An investor in oil and gas may be subject to the alternative minimum tax (AMT) as a result of the investment (see page 23). This possibility can arise mainly from two sources — the deduction for IDC on productive wells and the percentage depletion deduction.

Intangible drilling costs represent a tax preference item, but only within limits. Thus, it is only the amount by which "excess intangible drilling costs" exceeds net income from oil and gas properties that is a tax preference. Excess IDC is the amount by which the allowable IDC deduction on productive wells exceeds the amount that would have been deducted had the intangibles been capitalized and deducted on a straight-line basis over 10 years or had cost depletion been used. In determining net income for purposes of measuring the excess IDC, the total expenses attributable to oil and gas properties are reduced by the amount determined to be excess IDC and by all expenses, including dry hole costs, incurred on properties that have no gross income.

The percentage depletion deduction allowed to an oil and gas investor also can create a preference item. It is the amount by which percentage depletion on a property exceeds the property's tax basis that constitutes a preference. Thus, once a property's basis has been recovered through depletion, all subsequent percentage depletion is a tax preference item.

Under the AMT rules, individual taxpayers may remove IDC from the AMTI by electing to capitalize such costs and recover them through amortization over five or 10 years, depending upon the form of the taxpayer's investment.

The five-year recovery option (available for wells in the United States) is available only for those IDC deductions of individuals that are not incurred through a limited partnership. If an election is made to capitalize IDC under this option, the costs qualify for the investment tax credit at the 10% rate. Recovery of costs, which begins in the year the costs are incurred, is allowed under the following schedule:

Taxable Year	Percentage of Costs
First year	15
Second year	22
Third year	21
Fourth year	21
Fifth year	21

An individual may also remove the tax preference taint from IDC incurred as a limited partner in a limited partnership. Under this option, the capitalized IDC are recoverable ratably over 10 years, beginning with the year the costs are incurred. Unlike costs capitalized under the five-year recovery option, costs capitalized under the 10-year recovery option do not qualify for the investment tax credit.

An individual also is allowed to capitalize under the 10-year recovery option IDC that are not incurred through a limited partnership. Except in the case of non-U.S. wells, this option appears to be of little or no practical value in view of the more liberal five-year recovery period, which carries with it qualification for the investment credit.

IDC that have been deducted under any of the options discussed above are subject to the IDC recapture rules upon disposition of the property on which they were incurred (see page 61); the investment tax credit recapture rules also apply (see page 19).

The IDC tax preference rules impose additional tax planning burdens on investors in oil and gas activities. The advantages gained by eliminating IDC from a tax preference status and perhaps qualifying the deduction for the investment credit must be weighed against the disadvantage of spreading the deduction over five or 10 years. This evaluation entails consideration of many factors, including immediate reduction of the AMT, use of the additional investment tax credit that capitalization of IDC may generate, present value of future tax benefits from amortization, etc.

Windfall profit tax. In addition to the AMT, participation in oil and gas activities may also subject an investor to the Crude Oil Windfall Profit Tax (WPT). This is an excise tax imposed at various rates on the excess of the removal price (generally the same as the selling price) of domestic crude oil over a base price (as adjusted). The chief purpose of the WPT is to prevent the realization of "windfall" profits by producers as a result of the deregulation of domestic crude oil prices.

The WPT is based on a complex system of rates involving a three-tier classification of crude oil, each tier taxable at a different rate. The first and second tiers provide for a reduced rate of tax for a limited quantity of oil produced by independent producers, a category for which most shelter investors qualify. The third tier tax, imposed on "newly discovered oil" and certain other oil, is the one with which a new tax shelter investor in oil probably will be most concerned. (Appendix E summarizes the three-tier WPT rates.)

The WPT is deductible by a taxpayer in determining taxable income for income tax purposes; the amount of windfall profit on which the WPT is imposed is limited to 90% of net income (as defined) from crude oil.

At-risk rules. Unlike investments in real estate, the at-risk rules discussed in Chapter 2 rest heavily upon the investor in oil and gas. Thus, an oil and gas investor may only deduct losses from oil and gas activities up to the total of the investor's investment of money or other property and the indebtedness incurred with respect to the oil and gas activities for which the investor is *personally* liable. Other debt (nonrecourse debt) incurred in connection with the activity may be considered at risk for this purpose only if the investor has secured it with personal assets not used in the activity. It is the tax basis of those assets, not their fair market value, that determines the extent to which such debt is considered to put the investor at risk.

In applying the at-risk rules to oil and gas operations, percentage depletion in excess of tax basis is considered to be an amount at risk. This gratuitous increase in the amount at risk allows an oil and gas investor to deduct losses resulting from the percentage depletion allowance that otherwise might have been limited by the general at-risk requirements. This treatment is consistent with the inherent artificiality of the percentage depletion deduction and its allowance through "legislative grace." This provision is of great benefit to an investor, since the depletion deduction may represent a substantial part of the loss incurred in oil and gas operations.

Losses disallowed by the at-risk rules are not lost permanently as a deduction; they may be carried over and deducted in a subsequent year when the investor has a sufficient amount at risk to absorb them. Conversely, however, the initial allowance of a loss under the at-risk rules does not permanently secure it; it subsequently may be recaptured or restored to income should the investor's at-risk position deteriorate to the point at which accumulated losses exceed it.

The Importance of Planning

The importance of planning for an investor in oil and gas operations cannot be overemphasized. The various rules that limit the current use of losses and credits, create ordinary income through recapture, and subject the investor to the alternative minimum tax create a maze whose intricacies can trap the unwary. And these complexities are magnified because the effects of these factors may extend beyond the activity from which they arise to encompass other components of a taxpayer's total tax position.

Types of Oil and Gas Investments

An investor may participate in oil and gas activities generally in two ways. The investor can do so indirectly (as is most commonly done) through investment in a limited partnership. Alternatively, the investor can do so directly by acquiring a fractional, undivided working interest in a co-owned oil and gas property.

Co-Ownership

An investor may participate in oil and gas activities through co-ownership of the properties, although that method of participation is not available to most investors. Opportunities to participate in such arrangements generally arise from personal acquaintance with an independent oil and gas operator; participation usually involves an investment of a greater amount of funds, time and effort than most investors are willing to commit.

Co-ownership means simply that the investor directly owns a fractional, undivided working interest in the investment properties. As a result, the co-owner/investor participates in every item of income and expense attributable to each property in accordance with the fraction of ownership. Responsibility for the actual operation of each property is vested in one of the co-owners (called the operator) by execution of an operating agreement by all the co-owners.

Even though a co-ownership arrangement legally may not be a partnership, it may well be considered a partnership for income tax purposes and thus be subject to the tax rules that apply to partnerships and their partners. If that result is not desired by the co-owners, however, they may "elect out" of the partnership tax provisions and be treated for tax purposes as individual owners. To elect to do so, however, requires that certain conditions be met, most notably the retention by the co-owners of the right to take in kind their share of production (that is, oil and gas produced by the property).

One of the legal advantages that co-ownership offers over partnership arrangements is that such interests generally are more easily transferable than partnership interests; additionally, co-ownership interests generally have a greater value as collateral than do partnership interests. Co-ownership also allows an investor to make personal elections on various tax matters, rather than having them made at the partnership level.

The principal disadvantage of co-ownership is that the co-owner/investor does not enjoy the limited liability available under a limited partnership arrangement, a significant difference that makes co-ownership unattractive to most tax shelter investors. Another significant disadvantage is that co-ownership ordinarily does not allow as much flexibility as does a limited partnership to make special allocations of costs among the investors. However, the joint operating agreement among the co-owners perhaps may be written to effect the desired tax results.

Limited Partnership

The limited partnership is the vehicle through which most shelter investors participate in oil and gas operations. Aside from its inherent merit of limiting the investor's liability, the partnership form offers the opportunity for making special allocations of costs that benefit the investor through maximizing personal tax deductions. These allocations are discussed below.

Publicly Traded Limited Partnership

Another form of oil and gas investment that has gained recent popularity is the publicly traded limited partnership. Although not typically considered a tax shelter, this form of investment combines the general characteristics of the limited partnership investment with some sheltering of taxes though special provisions allowing for the recovery of the investment through cost depletion deductions; it also offers increased liquidity, due to the freely transferable nature of this investment.

Sharing Arrangements

The term "sharing arrangement" is used to denote the agreement among general and limited partners of a limited partnership that determines how revenues and costs are to be shared by the partners. Such an arrangement may involve the allocation of tax deductible costs to the limited partners and capital costs to the general partners. Such allocations cannot be contrived; they must have substantial economic effect if they are to stand for tax purposes.

Although there are many types of sharing arrangements, they generally are classified within one of the following categories:

☐ Functional allocation of costs.

☐ Promoted interest (disproportionate sharing).

☐ Carried interest.

☐ Reversionary interest.

Functional Allocation

The functional allocation of costs is a sharing arrangement commonly used in oil and gas limited partnerships. Under this arrangement, costs that must be capitalized for federal income tax purposes are paid by the general partner; whereas costs that are deductible as incurred are paid by the limited partners. This method of cost allocation is also known as the tangible/intangible method of allocation. The general partner participates in revenues from the very beginning, the extent of that participation depending on the agreement among the partners. The level of participation is, however, generally substantial, perhaps as high as 40%; sometimes it is higher.

Although this arrangement does maximize the tax deductions of the limited partners, it also maximizes risk, since the limited partners must bear the full cost of dry holes and most of the cost of drilling productive wells.

Promoted Interest

In this sharing arrangement, the general partner's share in the revenues exceeds the participation in costs. This excess of revenue participation over cost participation is the "promoted" interest, and it can be substantial. In such cases, it is not unusual for the general partner to pay as little as 10% of the costs for a 25% participation in the revenues.

Carried Interest

A carried interest sharing arrangement is one in which the general partner participates substantially in revenues from inception (perhaps an average of 12% or even more), while bearing a minimal share of costs (perhaps 1%). Thus, the general partner's costs are borne substantially, or "carried," by the limited partners. Once the limited partners have recouped their costs (referred to as "payout") from their share of production, the general partner's income interest may increase a few more percentage points, rising to perhaps an average of 16% of income.

This sharing arrangement may take various forms. For example, the general partner may in some cases be carried only for the cost of drilling the first (exploratory) well on a prospect; thereafter, the general partner participates fully in the cost of drilling subsequent (development) wells.

Reversionary Interest

The reversionary-interest method of sharing costs and revenues involves a minimal participation in both costs and revenues (perhaps 1%) by the general partner until the limited partners have recovered their costs from revenues. After payout to the limited partners, the general partner's nominal interest reverts to a substantial interest, perhaps as much as 25%.

Is One Better Than Another?

An investor might logically ask if one of the above sharing arrangements is better than any other. Unfortunately, there is no ready answer to that question. Under any arrangement, the investor must be concerned with the tax benefits, which ordinarily means *maximum* tax benefits. Thus, the investor has no particular desire to invest in capital costs, preferring instead a deduction for intangibles. Any offering that an investor considers must be responsive to that requirement. It is important, for example, for the investor to determine who pays certain capital costs such as organization expenses, including sales commissions.

On the other hand, an investor must take into consideration that certain capital costs also yield tax benefits. An investment in lease and well equipment, for example, yields an investment tax credit equal to a portion of its cost (generally 8%-10%); the recovery of that cost under the ACRS rules offers further benefits over a relatively short recovery period of five years.

The broader question of whether a sharing arrangement is fair to the limited partners probably must be answered by reference to whether the level of participation by the general partner in revenues and costs is reasonable. The answer can be obtained in part by comparing a particular offering with other similar offerings and in part by seeking the expert opinion an adviser who is familiar with the usual terms of such offerings.

Ultimately, like any other shelter investment, a sharing arrangement must be measured against the investment standards of risk and reward. Thus, an investor must decide whether the risks to be assumed under a particular sharing arrangement are commensurate with the possible rewards that such a sharing arrangement offers.

Types of Partnership Programs

Several types of oil and gas drilling partnerships are available to investors; each investor can pick and choose among them for the type of program that best suits personal tax and financial requirements. Oil and gas partnership programs are generally classified within one of the following categories:

☐ Exploratory drilling partnership.

☐ Developmental drilling partnership.

☐ Balanced drilling partnership.

Exploratory Drilling Partnership

An exploratory drilling partnership exposes the investor to greater risks than any other, but it also offers the greatest potential rewards. This type of program involves either the search for new reserves of oil and gas on unproved acreage or the attempt to significantly extend the outer limits of a proved field. Exploratory drilling may also involve the drilling of deep wells to test whether oil or gas may lie in deeper zones than the one from which oil or gas is produced currently. Such exploratory programs obviously are burdened with great risk of failure. On the other hand, should the drilling result in the discovery of a new field or production zone, the rewards can be far in excess of the cost of drilling. A successful exploratory program offers potential for significant capital gain, since proved oil and gas properties can be sold rather than held for production of the reserves.

Because of its high degree of risk, an exploratory drilling program should be participated in only by the investor who is able and willing to suffer a total loss of the investment.

Developmental Drilling Partnership

Participation in a developmental drilling program is the safest means of investing in oil and gas tax shelters, but it also promises the least reward. This type of program involves the drilling of developmental wells, those which produce oil and gas from fields of reserves that have previously been proved by exploratory drilling. Since at the time such wells are drilled there is a reasonable expectation that they will be productive, such wells do not involve the high degree of risk that accompanies exploratory drilling. Their record of success is high, perhaps as much as 80%.

The cost of acquiring leases in proved areas generally is relatively high when compared with lease costs in unproved areas. This creates a tax disadvantage that must be considered by the investor, since such costs must be recovered through depletion. When a property qualifies for percentage depletion, the investor effectively derives no tax benefit from those leasehold costs. (When a proved property is transferred, the transferee generally is precluded from claiming percentage depletion on the property.)

Balanced Drilling Partnership

This type of program seeks to strike a balance between exploratory drilling and developmental drilling; accordingly, such a partnership participates in the drilling of both types of wells. Just as the risk is mixed, so is the potential for reward.

Other Factors

Other factors enter into oil and gas investments that may be no less important than those previously discussed. These factors are not tax-oriented considerations, but rather are items that should be taken into account by any prudent investor before an investment decision is made. To a large extent, these matters can be covered by thoroughly reading the prospectus or offering memorandum, or by consulting with advisers who are experienced in oil and gas investments and knowledgeable about the considerations that are important to such investments.

The Working Interest

As previously noted (see page 56), the working interest in an oil and gas property differs from the various passive interests; in summary, the working interest is burdened with all costs that must be incurred to explore and develop a property, but participates in revenues only to some lesser extent. The income shares reserved to royalty interests, overriding royalty interests, net profits interests, etc. can materially reduce an oil and gas drilling partnership's participation in the gross income from production. It is prudent for an investor to determine the extent to which the working interests of the partnership participates in the gross income produced from its drilling activities. There is no one standard against which that participation can be measured, but an investor must be satisfied that the level of participation is reasonable.

Conflicts of Interest

The potential for conflicts of interest between the general partner and the limited partners in an oil and gas drilling partnership must be recognized and accepted by an investor prior to the investment. In many cases, this potential for conflict is unavoidable, since the general partner ordinarily is engaged in other oil and gas operations. The general partner's activities may include (directly or through related parties) sponsoring other drilling partnerships, personally exploring for oil and gas, operating a drilling company or oil well service company, etc.

Every prospectus or offering memorandum should include a section describing possible conflicts of interest; an investor needs to read this information carefully before making an investment decision.

Track Record

Perhaps in no other shelter investment is the record of experience of the general partner more important than in oil and gas investments. The reason for this is obvious — the risk normally associated with oil and gas investments. Thus, an investor should learn as much as is practical about the general partner, including the general partner's experience in the industry and the results achieved by sponsorship of other partnerships. Here, too, a careful review of the prospectus or offering memorandum is essential; other inquiries, through business or financial sources, may be desirable.

Although a successful track record on the part of the general partner is generally very important in evaluating an oil and gas investment, such a record is not always determinative. Other factors an investor deems important may affect the relative significance of the general partner's track record.

Additional Assessments

The terms of some oil and gas drilling partnerships provide for assessment of the limited partners for additional capital contributions. Such additional capital may be required in an exploratory drilling partnership, for example, to provide funds for drilling developmental wells. There is nothing wrong with such assessments, so long as a limited partner understands at the time of the original investment that each such partner may be called upon to commit additional capital to the venture. Such possibility is particularly important, since an investor who fails to make additional contributions when called upon to do so normally will be subject to certain penalties that may reduce substantially the potential for gain on the investment.

Letters of credit. Additional commitments to an oil and gas program may be made through the use of letters of credit. In this type of arrangement, the investor obtains from a bank a letter authorizing the investor to draw on the bank for a specified sum; the bank guarantees acceptance of such drafts if the investor makes them. Although the investor does not initially draw on the letters of credit, the letters are used by the partnership as security for bank loans made to the partnership in order to finance the drilling of wells. It may be hoped, or even anticipated, that revenues from successful wells will be sufficient to liquidate the partnership debt without ever requiring the investor to draw on the letter of credit. If sufficient revenues are not forthcoming, however, the bank holding the letters as collateral for the partnership loan may cause the investors to draw on the letters of credit in order to retire the debt.

Using letters of credit in an oil and gas investment is a perfectly legitimate financing arrangement. However, an investor who uses that form of financing must realize that letters of credit are more than a means of obtaining tax deductions that exceed the amount that is directly invested in a partnership; the investor is *truly at risk* for such amounts. Were that not so, the at-risk rules would deny the investor tax losses that result from such financing.

There are some restrictions on the use of borrowings similar to the letter of credit arrangement described above, particularly if the borrowings are used to finance prepaid drilling costs.

Liquidity

A natural concern of most investors is the liquidity of their investments. Although most oil and gas tax shelter investments are not readily marketable, a recent innovation has provided a means for converting such investments into a more liquid form.

Under these "swap deals," a newly organized public corporation exchanges shares of its stock for diverse oil and gas interests on a basis that is intended to be taxfree to both parties. (The Internal Revenue Service, however, will not issue a private ruling on the tax consequences of those transactions.) In addition to providing marketability to the oil and gas investor who participates in the swap, the transaction frees the investor from possibly realizing ordinary income — from recapture of IDC and depreciation previously deducted — that would result from a taxable disposition of oil and gas interests.

An obvious requisite to such a swap transaction is that the investor's oil and gas interests be valued at an amount the investor believes to be fair. Once that hurdle is cleared, an investor must be willing to accept the fact that the future value of the stock depends on the fluctuations of the stock market, which may have little correlation with the value of the reserves in the ground that the original investment represented.

As discussed earlier, the publicly traded limited partnership investment provides an unusual degree of flexibility due to the liquidity of this type of investment. In recent instances, units of publicly traded limited partnerships have been exchanged in lieu of stock in "swap deals." It should be noted that the future value of units of a publicly traded limited partnership are also subject to the fluctuations of the marketplace.

Equipment Leasing

Leasing is a technique commonly used by business to finance a wide range of personal property such as airplanes, computers, railroad rolling stock, drilling rigs, vessels, etc. Historically, the tax law has made such leasing transactions highly desirable, allowing various tax benefits — derived from depreciation and interest deductions and the investment tax credit — to be used by high-bracket investors/lessors who could, as a result, offer lower financing costs to business lessees.

The suitability of equipment leasing as a tax shelter investment for individual investors depends basically on three tax attributes — the depreciation deduction, the interest expense deduction and the investment tax credit. With respect to these, recent tax developments have been somewhat ambiguous toward leasing transactions. Thus, the liberal cost recovery provisions of the ACRS rules allow more rapid recovery of the cost of leased equipment; whereas the at-risk rules make it more difficult to use the losses and investment credits that arise from leasing transactions. On balance, equipment leasing is still a tax shelter vehicle that merits consideration by shelter investors.

Leasing in General

Equipment leasing is an established, vital factor in our economic system; it is responsible for the financing of a significant part of the nation's capital expenditures. Lease financing is offered by various lessors, including independent, captive and specialized leasing companies. Sophisticated lease packages are offered by lease underwriters or brokers, investment bankers, finance companies and commercial banks. Such lease packages usually cover "big-ticket" items such as aircraft, railroad rolling stock, ships and vessels, oil drilling rigs, computers, public utility property, and complete industrial plants. Manufacturers have frequently used leasing transactions to finance equipment acquisitions by their customers.

A variety of equipment lease contracts have been developed over time, each allowing the lessee to use the equipment in return for periodic rental payments over a specified period; however, a lease generally is classified either as a finance (full payout) lease or as an operating (non-full payout) lease.

The Finance Lease

Finance leases give the lessor full recovery of cost and a reasonable profit from rentals over the original noncancellable lease term. These leases provide certain tax benefits and may be leveraged or nonleveraged. In a leveraged lease, the lessor finances a significant portion (typically up to 80%) of the cost of the equipment through a nonrecourse loan. Under the terms of a nonrecourse loan, the lenders look to the equipment and a pledge of the lease payments as the sole security for their loan; they cannot look to other assets of the lessor. In the case of a nonleveraged lease, the lessor provides 100% of the equipment cost either entirely through equity or by a combination of equity and recourse debt. Finance leases are almost invariably net leases; that is, the lessee is obligated to pay for the expenses associated with the equipment — such as maintenance, insurance and property taxes — in addition to the rent which covers the actual cost of financing the equipment.

The return. Lessors have found that finance leases may provide attractive returns on their investment in relation to the risks assumed. The returns earned by a lessor under such leases are often higher than the returns that would be earned by a lender because the lessor's return comes partially from tax benefits and the value of the equipment at the termination of the lease (the "residual value"). Dependence on tax benefits and residuals for part of the return involves the assumption of additional risk by the lessor and is generally justified by higher returns.

When analyzing a prospective lease transaction, an investor/lessor typically uses conservative estimates of the residual value of the equipment. Although the residual value may offer some potential for gain and some hedge against inflation, it generally does not have a major impact on the expected yield. Therefore, leasing does not offer the same potential for gain that an investment in oil and gas, real estate, or timber generally is considered to offer investors.

Lessors generally calculate their anticipated return by analyzing the after-tax cash inflows and outflows from the lease transaction. Typically, the equipment purchase requires a large cash outflow at the inception of the lease. This is followed by cash inflows during the early term of the lease from lease rentals, tax deferrals resulting from tax losses created principally by accelerated depreciation, and tax savings from the investment tax credit. (However, the investment credit may not always be available to individual lessors.) There are cash outflows to pay taxes in the later part of the lease as the tax deferral reverses and, finally, a cash inflow from sale of the property at the end of the lease.

To adequately appraise a potential equipment leasing investment, the lessor must understand and evaluate each assumption on which the lease proposal is based. This is essential, for example, because very slight modifications in the timing of cash receipts and disbursements can significantly change the yield to the lessor. Other critical factors that affect an investor's return are the tax rate against which losses are used, the interest rate at which tax deferrals can be reinvested during the periods of positive cash flow, and the rate at which the deferred income ultimately is taxed.

The risks. The major risks to a lessor in finance lease arrangements are:

☐ Lessee's credit — Will the lessee be financially able to meet its lease payments? Is there sufficient collateral to cover that risk?

☐ Tax benefits — Has the lessor properly structured the transaction to obtain the tax benefits? Will there be sufficient taxable income to currently utilize all of the benefits? Will the tax law and the lessor's tax status remain as projected so that both the timing and the amount of tax savings and payments will be realized? What are the tax and financial results if the lessee defaults? What if the property is destroyed by fire or other natural disaster?

☐ Interest rate — The lessor essentially is extending credit throughout the lease term at a fixed rate, while the funds borrowed to finance the lease may be subject to varying rates.

☐ Residual value — Will the property be worth at least the anticipated amount at the end of the lease term?

☐ Drafting deficiencies — Is the lease document properly drafted to ensure that the lessor is protected by the lessee against losses, to the extent appropriate?

The Operating Lease

Unlike a finance lease, an operating lease does not provide the lessor with a full return of the equipment cost over the initial, noncancellable lease term. To ultimately realize a profit on an operating lease, the lessor must sell or re-lease the equipment profitably at the end of the initial lease term. An operating lease may or may not be a net lease. It is not unusual for lessors writing operating leases to provide other services, such as maintenance and repairs, along with the equipment. Such agreements may be written as leases or as operating contracts, and can be for periods as short as days or weeks, or as long as several years.

The return. The prior discussion of the return on a finance lease also generally pertains to an operating lease. An additional factor that enters into the return on an operating lease, however, is that some estimate must be made of the terms of a new lease after the initial lease's expiration, or, alternatively, the proceeds that can be realized from a sale of the property at that time. In the case of a sale, any recapture of investment credit also must be considered.

The risks. An operating lease is a much riskier transaction for a lessor than is a finance lease. To obtain a profit, the lessor must be able to sell or re-lease the equipment at the right price at the end of the original lease term. The lessor therefore risks loss from obsolescence of the equipment, lack of demand, or unfavorable lease terms. To compensate the lessor for this risk, lease rates for operating leases generally are significantly higher than rates for finance leases.

From the Lessee's Standpoint

Lessees view leasing as an alternative to the purchase of property. There are many reasons for leasing rather than purchasing equipment, such as 100% financing of the equipment, medium-term financing at fixed rates, the ability to acquire new equipment that cannot be purchased directly because of loan or budget restrictions, "off-balance-sheet" financing (although somewhat restricted by accounting rules), expansion of credit sources, etc. However, the most important reason for preferring leasing to purchasing is that leasing permits more efficient use of the tax incentives related to ownership of personal property — deferral of tax through depreciation and interest deductions, and tax savings provided by the investment tax credit. The availability of these incentives to the lessor enables the lessee to obtain the use of property under terms more favorable than those the lessor could have granted without these benefits.

The depreciation incentive has been enhanced by ACRS, which provides greater depreciation deductions in the early years of an asset's depreciable life than in later years, and allows depreciation of an asset over a period that often is shorter than its useful economic life. The economic benefit of these tax incentives enables a lessor to accept a lower return from rentals paid by the lessee than would otherwise be required.

Lessees should compare the after-tax cash flows of leasing to alternative methods of financing. In doing so, lessees should consider, as a part of the cost of leasing, the loss of the tax benefits of ownership and the fact that they will not own the equipment at the end of the lease. For short-term leases, this latter factor may be quite important; for long-term leases, it tends to be less so, since the present value of the residual generally is small.

A Basic Question

In a leasing transaction, the tax incentives associated with the ownership of property go to the lessor, not to the lessee. Although this may not be the sole (or even the primary) reason for entering into a lease transaction, tax incentives are factors that must be taken into account in calculating the lessor's return on investment. In doing so, however, the lessor must be relatively sure of obtaining these benefits. That assurance requires a determination of whether the lease is to be treated as a lease, a sale, or a financing transaction for tax purposes.

Whether a transaction is a lease, a sale, or a mere financing transaction has been the subject of considerable litigation between taxpayers and the government; it also is a matter on which the Internal Revenue Service has issued guidelines — criteria on which its policy for issuing rulings on leasing transactions is based.

The following general guidelines provided by court decisions may help to distinguish between leases and sales.

There is a substantial risk that a transaction will *not* be treated as a lease under any of the following circumstances:

☐ Where the lessee is given a purchase option at a nominal amount, or at an amount that is less than the expected fair market value of the property.

☐ Where the lessee is given the right to continue using the property after the initial lease term for less than a fair market rental rate and the renewal term, plus the initial lease term, extends for substantially all of the useful life of the property.

☐ Where the lease term essentially equals the economic life of the property.

☐ Where the property will have nominal value at the end of the lease term.

It is also quite important that the lessor have a reasonable expectation of realizing an economic profit from a leasing transaction — a profit apart from the associated tax benefits. If the *only* purpose of entering into the transaction is to save taxes, it may be treated as a sham by the Internal Revenue Service, thus denying the tax benefits to the lessor. Under such circumstances, a lessor could also incur substantial penalties as a result of the transaction (see page 28).

Tax Benefits

As was noted earlier, the three tax legs upon which most equipment leasing transactions stand are:

☐ Depreciation deduction.

☐ Interest deduction.

☐ Investment tax credit.

Depreciation

Under the ACRS rules, the cost of personal property (other than certain public utility property) is recoverable over three, five or 10 years at accelerated rates (see Appendix A). Most property underlying equipment lease transaction qualifies for the five-year recovery period. This depreciation period is allowed without regard to either the term of the lease or the expected economic life of the equipment.

Interest

Most leased property is financed at least partially by debt. Although the interest on such debt generally is deductible, the amount deductible in a net lease transaction is subject to limitation (see page 79).

Investment Credit

Property with an ACRS recovery period of five years or more qualifies for the maximum 10% investment credit. Thus, the cost of leased property generally yields the lessor an immediate tax credit of 10% of that cost, subject to the at-risk requirements (see page 77) and the basis reduction rules (see page 18).

Limitations

Congress has reduced the tax incentives for individual and other noncorporate lessors such as partnerships by:

☐ Limiting the deductible loss attributable to leased property and the investment tax credit on such property to an amount for which the taxpayer is at risk.

☐ Classifying depreciation in excess of straight-line depreciation as an item of tax preference.

☐ Classifying the interest cost of financing equipment subject to a net lease as investment interest expense generally subject to a $10,000 interest deduction limitation.

☐ Effectively denying the investment tax credit to noncorporate lessors in many leasing situations.

At-Risk Limitations

The allowable loss attributable to leased property is limited by the amount for which the taxpayer is at risk. In general, the amount at risk includes the money and recourse indebtedness (if any) used to acquire the equipment. The limitation is applied on a property-by-property basis; thus, amounts at risk relating to one item of leased property cannot increase the amounts at risk for other properties. Most individual investors in leases, however, probably invest through limited partnerships, in which case their status under the at-risk rules is determined by the aggregate of their investment and the debt for which they are personally liable. The limitation is applicable to all depreciable tangible personal property and depreciable real property (except buildings and their structural components) used in certain specified activities. The at-risk limitation generally applies to all leases (net leases, finance leases, operating leases, etc.) of personal property by noncorporate lessors, S corporations, and certain closely held corporations. This limitation may not be too burdensome where a lessee has a good credit rating that makes it feasible for the lessor to assume personal liability for the debt. Even so, however, an investor may understandably be reluctant to make such a commitment.

The basis of property eligible for investment tax credit must be reduced by the amount of nonrecourse financing (other than allowable commercial financing) attributable to that property. Qualified commercial financing includes financing other than convertible debt that is provided or guaranteed by any government entity, or borrowed from a qualified person. A qualified person is an unrelated party that is actively and regularly engaged in the business of lending money. In order for the exception for qualified commercial financing to apply, the amount of nonrecourse financing applicable to the property may not exceed 80% of the credit base.

To illustrate this, assume a partnership purchases equipment for $1,000,000, of which $200,000 is a cash down payment and $800,000 is borrowed on a nonrecourse basis from a local bank. *The entire $1,000,000 cost qualifies for investment credit* since 20% of the purchase price consisted of cash (at-risk investment) and the remainder, although nonrecourse, was borrowed from an independent bank (a qualified lender).

Investment credits originally limited under the at-risk rules can later be used when nonrecourse debt is subsequently paid. Thus, to the extent that the principal amount of nonrecourse debt is reduced, investment credit can be claimed on this principal reduction even though it did not occur in the year that the underlying qualified investment credit property was placed in service.

An exception to the at-risk rules that limit losses exempts from those rules the leasing of equipment by certain closely held corporations whose principal activity is equipment leasing. This exception is of no benefit, however, to individual lessors.

Recapture. Investment credits originally qualifying under the at-risk rules must be recaptured should the taxpayer's at-risk amount subsequently be reduced. The extent of the recapture is determined by the extent to which the taxpayer ceases to be at risk for indebtedness or reduces the original at-risk investment. Although recapture is computed as if the reduced at-risk amounts were in existence at the time the qualified property was placed in service, the recapture tax is actually due for the year in which the reduction in the at-risk amount occurs. The transfer of a nonrecourse debt from a qualified lender to a related party does not constitute a reduction in the at-risk amount if such a transfer occurs after one year from the original date of the loan.

Denial of Investment Credit

Noncorporate lessors and S corporation lessors are not entitled to the investment tax credit even if the at-risk rules are satisfied *unless* either:

☐ The equipment has been manufactured or produced by the lessor in the ordinary course of business, or

☐ The equipment is leased for less than 50% of its useful life and the ordinary and necessary business expenses (other than depreciation, interest, taxes, and certain other expenses) attributable to the first 12 months of the lease exceed 15% of the rental income attributable to that period.

In the case of the individual investor, the first requirement for earning the investment credit is usually difficult enough to meet, since an investor is unlikely to manufacture or produce the property. The 15% test in the alternative requirement may be equally unattainable, since the main expenses associated with the typical lease are nonqualifying expenses — depreciation, interest and taxes. The remaining expenses usually inherent in a lease are insurance, maintenance, and management fees; for many types of equipment, the sum of these latter expenses that are attributable to the first 12 months of the lease will not exceed 15% of the rents. The requirement that the lease be short-term imposes additional burdens on the investor, since it increases the uncertainty of the economic results of the transaction. In a recent case, the parties expected to continue leasing the property (by either extending the lease or negotiating a new lease) beyond the stated end of the lease; the court held that this expected longer lease term violated the 50% test stated above.

In summary, noncorporate lessors desiring the investment tax credit are required to take greater risks. They must pay certain of the operating expenses not ordinarily assumed by a lessor and generally must either re-lease or sell the equipment for a substantial amount at the end of the short lease term in order to realize an economic profit from the transaction.

If the property being leased is new, individual lessors can elect to pass on the investment credit to the lessee, whether or not the above tests are met. However, in order to obtain the full credit, the lessee must be at risk for rental payments with a present value equal to at least 30% of the lessee's investment tax credit basis (18% in the case of three-year property) Such a pass-through of the credit should warrant an adjustment to the rental rate that otherwise would apply, thus making the transaction economically feasible for the lessor and providing one possible solution to the difficulties imposed on individuals who want to get the benefits of the investment credit but are precluded from doing so directly.

Tax Preference

For noncorporate lessors of personal property, S corporations and personal holding companies, an AMT preference item may arise from depreciation deductions on leased property. The preference item is the amount by which the ACRS depreciation deductions exceed the straight-line depreciation deductions that would have been allowed using recovery periods as follows:

ACRS Classification	Recovery Period
3-year property	5 years
5-year property	8 years
10-year property	15 years
15-year public utility property	22 years

Interest Expense Limitation

For individuals and S corporations, the deductibility of investment interest expense is generally limited to the sum of the following:

□ $10,000.

□ The amount of the taxpayer's net investment income.

□ The amount by which the deductions for ordinary and necessary business expenses, interest and taxes attributable to property of the taxpayer subject to a net lease exceed the rental income from the property for the taxable year.

In computing the above amount, property subject to a net lease is considered to be property held for investment; the related interest expense is treated as investment interest expense which is subject to this limitation. Property is treated as subject to a net lease if, for the taxable year, the sum of the ordinary and necessary business expenses — other than interest, depreciation, taxes, and certain other expenses — is less than 15% of the rental income, or the lessor is either guaranteed a specified return or is guaranteed, in whole or in part, against loss of income.

Types of Leasing Investments

A shelter investor who chooses to use leasing as a means for achieving shelter goals can select among a myriad of leasing opportunities. These opportunities generally can be categorized as follows:

□ Separate and full ownership of a specific leased asset by the investor, who pools the asset with those of other investors; this arrangement is commonly used for containers, rail cars, and trailers.

□ A partnership with a single big-ticket asset, such as an airplane.

□ A partnership with multiple assets subject to finance and/or operating leases. The assets may be of different types or may be units of the same type, such as containers.

□ A "blind" partnership, in which the type of asset to be invested in and the type of lease to be entered into are determined subsequent to the partners' investments.

One characteristic that these arrangements share is a need for a manager, operator or general partner to run the leasing activities. Not surprisingly, this requires the payment of compensation such as management fees, the sharing of income and losses, the sharing of the residual value of the assets, and perhaps a fee for marketing the equipment at the appropriate time. Care should be taken to ensure that the management contract does not constitute either a lease or a partnership as this could alter (or even eliminate) some of the tax results.

Leasing to a Related Corporation

When a corporation cannot fully utilize all of the tax benefits associated with an equipment acquisition, it is not unusual for the stockholders to consider acquiring the equipment and leasing it to the corporation. This arrangement can be particularly attractive, since the value of the tax benefits can be realized without giving up the residual value of the property to "outsiders." Unfortunately, the investment tax credit in such an arrangement was recently disallowed on the basis that the lease, in fact, had an indefinite term and therefore did not meet the requirement that the term run for less than 50% of the useful life of the property.

A stockholder contemplating such an arrangement should carefully review relevant court decisions and position of the Internal Revenue Service before consummating the transaction. Care should also be taken to ensure that the terms of the lease, including rental levels, are negotiated as arm's length transactions. As an alternative to retaining the credit, the stockholder may consider passing the credit through to the corporate lessee, retaining only the tax benefits of accelerated depreciation.

Other Equipment Transactions

In tax shelter investing, equipment transactions most often involve leasing; there are, however, other transactions, not strictly called leasing, that may be appropriate for shelter investments.

An example of this type of activity is the ownership and operation of onshore and/or offshore oil drilling rigs and other equipment affording the investor the same tax benefits as equipment leasing.

In these transactions, the investors' partnership uses the equipment to provide the service (such as drilling) rather than leasing it to another user for that purpose. This arrangement may avoid many of the special tax problems faced by a noncorporate lessor, such as the tax preferences on accelerated depreciation, the investment interest expense applicable to a net lease, and the special limitations that apply to investment tax credits. The business risks are usually quite similar to those incurred in leasing transactions.

Farming

Many investors have engaged in a variety of farming activities to achieve tax shelter goals. Changes in the tax law over the years and the current economics of farming, however, have dampened the enthusiasm of many investors for those activities. Even so, farming activities cannot be excluded from consideration as shelter opportunities, since careful adherence to the tax rules that apply to those activities may still result in significant deferral of income taxes.

The Business of Farming

Under federal tax rules, farming means "the cultivation of land or the raising or harvesting of any agricultural or horticultural commodity including the raising, shearing, feeding, caring for, training, and management of animals" That is indeed a wide variety of activity, thus, it is not surprising that U.S. farming activities produce annual revenues of approximately $150 billion.

As farm revenues have grown, so has the complexity of farming. With increased complexity have come demands for greater managerial and technical skills to implement and operate the vertically integrated farming activities known as "agribusiness." In the cattle industry, for example, a single agribusiness operation may not only feed and breed cattle, but may also grow the feed on which the cattle are raised and perhaps operate its own packing plants and distribution centers.

In spite of great advances in technology and productivity, prices commanded by farm products in recent years have not kept pace with the prices paid by farmers for goods and services required to produce those products. Farm net income has suffered badly as a result falling 28% from 1982 to 1983.

In today's economic climate, farming should be entered into with great caution, for the chances of economic loss are considerable. However, an investor must also realize that a farming venture can lead to other opportunities. In some cases, farming activities have provided a means for holding farmland until it could be adapted to a higher and better use. Such a development can yield capital gains that may significantly exceed any operating losses that may have been incurred.

The Tax Rules

The attractiveness of farming as a tax shelter investment before it was "tax reformed" was due to the fact that a farmer using the cash method of accounting could gain substantial tax benefits. For example, much of the costs incurred to develop farmlands and orchards and to raise certain livestock could be deducted as incurred, even though such costs increased the value of the assets on which they were expended. These deductions could be used (both by active, full-time farmers and by passive investors engaged in farming as a sideline to their principal occupations) to reduce or shelter ordinary income from other sources. In some cases, these deductions could be financed through loans for which the borrower may or may not have been personally liable.

A further incentive to participation in farming activities was the fact that the values created through tax-deductible expenditures and normal value increases could be realized through sales that resulted in capital gains taxable at favorable rates.

Much of that has changed. Farming is now subject to the at-risk rules that can deny the use of losses and investment credits; the depreciation recapture rules that can minimize capital gains; the special rules that apply to passive investors who engage in farming through limited partnerships, farming syndicates, or techniques deemed to be "tax shelters"; the special provisions that deny use of the favorable cash method of accounting in certain cases; etc. Moreover, certain corporations engaged in farming and partnerships with corporate partners are required to use the accrual method of accounting for the farming activity.

At-Risk Rules

The at-risk rules governing the allowance of losses from activities other than real estate have been discussed previously; the rules pertaining to the allowance of the investment tax credit were also discussed above (see page 22). Those at-risk rules also apply to farming activities.

Farming Syndicates

Special tax rules limit the extent to which deductions for feed, seed, fertilizer or similar farm supplies are allowed when incurred by "farming syndicates." Certain poultry expenses incurred by such organizations also are subject to special rules of deduction.

Syndicate. The definition of a farming syndicate is rather broad, seemingly designed to snare the passive, nonfarmer investor. Thus, a farming syndicate is *either* of the following:

☐ A partnership or any other enterprise (other than a regular corporation) engaged in farming that has offered interests in the entity in an offering required to be registered with any federal or state agency.

☐ A partnership or any other enterprise (other than a regular corporation) engaged in farming if more than 35% of losses during any period are allocable to limited partners or "limited entrepreneurs."

In the latter definition, a limited entrepreneur is any person who has an interest in the enterprise other than as a limited partner and who does not actively participate in the management of the entity.

Exceptions. For the 35% test that is part of the second definition above, there are various exceptions for certain individuals who might otherwise be considered limited partners or entrepreneurs. Basically, these exceptions apply only to individuals who are otherwise actively engaged in farming in various ways; they would not ordinarily apply to the passive, nonfarmer investor.

Farm supplies. The farming syndicate rules preclude the deduction of the cost of feed, seed, fertilizer and similar farm supplies until they are actually used or consumed, regardless of when such costs are actually paid.

Poultry expenses. Under the farming syndicate provisions, certain poultry expenses are singled out for special treatment:

☐ The cost of poultry, including egg-laying hens and baby chicks, that is purchased for use in the trade or business (or both for use and for sale) must be capitalized and deducted over the lesser of 12 months or their useful lives.

☐ The cost of poultry purchased for sale can be deducted only in the year sold or otherwise disposed of.

Tax Shelters

Even if the farming syndicate rules are avoided, if the farming investment is made through a partnership or as a direct investment which meets the definition of a "tax shelter" the above rules apply. Generally, a "tax shelter" is any arrangement where the principal purpose is the avoidance or evasion of federal income taxes.

Accounting Method

Farming was once a business that offered significant benefits from use of the cash method of accounting, under which expenses generally are deducted when paid and income recognized when received. Thus, the cost of planting crops or fattening animals could be deducted in one year to create losses while the income recognition lagged to a subsequent year when the crops or animals were sold.

The use of the cash method of accounting was available to all farmers, even large corporate organizations whose size belied the general notion of a "farmer." Congress apparently felt that it was inappropriate to allow such organizations to use the cash method of accounting in farming operations; accordingly, it created rules that generally require corporations and partnerships with corporate partners to use the accrual method of accounting to determine their taxable income.

Preproductive period expenses. The tax rules prescribing the accrual method of accounting also require that certain organizations capitalize rather than expense currently certain expenses incurred on farm property before it becomes productive. Such expenses include all expenses (other than taxes, interest, and costs incurred as a result of natural disasters) attributable to crops, animals, and any other farm property having a crop or yield during the preproductive period of the property.

In the case of property having a useful life of more than one year and which will have more than one crop or yield, the preproductive period within which costs must be capitalized is the period before the disposition of the first marketable crop or yield. In the case of any other property, the preproductive period is the period before the property is disposed of.

Exceptions. Excepted from the requirement that corporations and certain partnerships engaged in farming use the accrual method of accounting and capitalize preproductive period expenses are the following types of entities:

☐ Electing small business corporations.

☐ Corporations of which at least 50% of the stock is owned by members of the same family.

☐ Corporations having gross receipts of $1,000,000 or less in each prior taxable year.

☐ Entities engaged in the business of operating a nursery or sod farm, or raising or harvesting trees other than fruit or nut trees.

Citrus and Almond Groves

Citrus and almond groves have been singled out for special attention under the tax law. As a result, any amount that would otherwise be deductible under the tax rules must be capitalized if:

☐ Such amounts are attributable to the planting, cultivation, maintenance or development of a citrus or almond grove, *and*

☐ Such amounts are incurred before the close of the fourth taxable year beginning with the taxable year in which the citrus or almond trees were planted.

Farming syndicates. Farming syndicates (defined on page 83) are further restricted in deducting planting, cultivation, maintenance and development costs. For syndicates, such costs incurred for any grove, orchard or vineyard in which fruits or nuts are grown must be capitalized when incurred in any taxable year before the first taxable year in which the grove, orchard or vineyard bears a crop in commercial quantities.

Exceptions. None of these rules requiring capitalization of planting, cultivation, maintenance and development costs (including those for farming syndicates) applies to amounts that would ordinarily be deductible and that are incurred for replanting a grove, orchard or vineyard that was lost or damaged by reason of freezing temperatures, disease, drought, pests or casualty.

Excess Deductions Account

For a number of years the tax law contained a complex set of rules for what was known as the excess deductions account (EDA). Starting in 1976, there were no further additions to these accounts and the recapture provisions have been completely repealed for years beginning after December 31, 1983.

Other Farm Provisions

Other provisions in the tax law apply solely to farming, although they are less significant than those already discussed. For example, certain costs incurred for soil and water conservation that would otherwise be required to be capitalized are allowed to be expensed (within certain limits). Costs incurred in clearing land to make it suitable for farming may also be deducted (within certain limits) rather than capitalized. All of these costs, however, are subject to recapture as ordinary income if the land on which they are claimed is sold within 10 years of its acquisition, the extent of recapture depending on the holding period of the land.

There are also provisions that allow for the current deduction of the cost of fertilizer, lime, etc. that is used to enrich, neutralize or condition land used in farming.

Capital Gain

Gain or loss realized from the sale of livestock (held for draft, breeding, dairy or sporting purposes) or unharvested crops may receive the special treatment afforded to assets used in a trade or business. Thus, a gain may be treated as a capital gain, while a loss may be allowed as an ordinary deduction. Livestock must be held for at least 12 months (except cattle and horses, which must be held for 24 months) to qualify for capital gain treatment. Capital gain may also be realized from the sale of land owned and used in farming and held for more than 12 months; such gain may be realized on the unharvested crops on such land, if both the land and the unharvested crops are sold to the same person at the same time (with no right or option of reacquisition). The costs incurred in producing the unharvested crops, however, may not be deducted.

Certain exchanges of farm property may qualify for favorable tax treatment as exchanges of "like-kind" property held for "productive use or investment" (see page 47). However, exchanges of livestock of different sexes cannot qualify for that treatment.

Investment Tax Credit

Many farm-related assets qualify for the investment tax credit. In addition to the traditional machinery and equipment on which the credit is available, trees, vines, irrigation systems (including pumps and wells), fences, and special-purpose agricultural and horticultural buildings may qualify for the credit. All livestock (except horses) used for draft, breeding or dairy purposes also qualify for the credit.

Selected Farming Operations

Various types of farming operations have been popular with investors over the years. The popularity of those activities has declined, however, with the imposition of various strictures on farm deductions and losses, and with the deterioration of the economic potential of farming. Several of the more important of these activities still warrant discussion since, when properly structured, they may offer viable investment opportunities for the tax shelter investor.

Cattle Feeding

Cattle feeding has long been a popular shelter activity for investors. As a result of the at-risk rules, the farming syndicate rules, and the recent tax shelter rules of Tax Reform Act of 1984, cattle feeding is now impractical for most passive farm investors.

Cattle feeding or fattening involves the purchase of beef cattle at weights of approximately 650-700 pounds. These steers are then fed or fattened in feed lots until they attain weights of approximately 1,100 pounds, at which time they are sold for slaughter. Whether a profit is realized on the transaction depends on the costs incurred to fatten the cattle and the price at which they ultimately are sold. Any gain realized is treated as ordinary income; no capital gain can be realized from the sale of feeder cattle.

The tax benefits of cattle feeding involve the *deferral* of income. To achieve that deferral, most of the feeding costs must be incurred in one taxable year, with the proceeds from the sale of the cattle realized in the next year.

Although the great demand for beef makes cattle feeding a big business, the business is a risky one. To reap the maximum tax benefits, an investor must enter into the business directly (not through a farming syndicate), must be personally liable for any debt incurred in the feeding operation, and must be perceived as entering the transaction for a primary purpose other than tax avoidance. Although the business ensures tax deductions, the risk of economic loss is considerable.

Breeding Herds

Due to greater capital gain potential, some cattle investors have moved toward investments in commercial cattle breeding programs, which provide animals for both beef and dairy operations. Some investors have limited their investments to purebred breeding operations, which are generally higher-risk ventures.

As with feeders, the purchase of a breeding herd may be leveraged (a noncorporate investor, however, must be personally liable for the debt). Cattle programs accept an investment in as few as 50 to 100 animals. The after-tax outlay required of a 50%-bracket taxpayer for an initial breeding herd of 100 cattle may represent a substantial annual investment, generally for a period of five years.

The cattle are usually bred in the summer or fall, so the calves will drop in warm weather. A calf crop of 75% to 95% normally can be expected. After the calves are weaned, the steers are sold and the heifers are retained to build up the breeding herd. The new crop of heifers is generally bred at two years of age. Each year, certain animals are culled from the breeding herd and sold at capital gain rates if the animals are held for 24 or more months. Sales of steers result in ordinary income.

Technological advances in the field of embryo transplantation have brought about a new type of breeding program. Such programs usually consist of a relatively few prize breeding animals and a larger number of donor cows. Transplanting allows the genetic makeup of the female animal to be multiplied many times during the same time period that the prize cow would have required to carry a calf to birth. The advantages of producing a quality herd with fewer prize breeding stock, however, should be weighed against the relatively high cost of transplanting the embryo and the short track record for calving rates of such operations.

The cycle of a breeding herd investment is about five to seven years. At the end of that period, the herd should have grown considerably, the quality should have been established, and most of the costs to raise the animals should have been deducted currently as they were incurred. The sale of the raised breeding animals qualifies for capital gain treatment. Gain on sale of purchased breeding animals, however, must be recaptured as ordinary income to the extent depreciation has been claimed.

Combined Feeding and Breeding

Diversification in the form of a combined feeding and breeding operation provides for a longer-lasting investment. The yearly cycle of feeding is extended to a period that provides for the "building" of herds in hope of rising demand and/or prices. In a further attempt to minimize risks, increase liquidity, and generate immediate tax advantages, some farm investors are also beginning to invest in ventures that lease range land and confined feeding areas. Such arrangements stabilize the risk for the investor. These programs run for seven to ten years, and a purchase option on the land and feeding facilities is often available.

Rollover Programs

Another option for the high-bracket taxpayer is to participate in a rollover program involving annual field crops such as wheat, corn, soybeans or similar crops. The program consists of becoming a joint venturer with an established farmer, deducting a share of the fall planting and cultural costs, and recognizing income in the following year when the crop is harvested and sold. Commodities hedging may be used to reduce risks from falling prices. Depending on the perishability of the crop, the rollover can be extended to cover more than one year or can be used in combination with a breeding program. Such combination could provide cash flow to help offset the carrying costs of the herd.

Vineyards, Orchards and Groves

Investments in vineyards, orchards and groves by nonfarmers have been adversely affected by the requirement that preproductive period expenses be capitalized rather than expensed as incurred. These costs are significant, since the development of groves, orchards and vineyards can require a significant outlay of funds over the first four to six years. During this period, the land is acquired and prepared for planting, and irrigation and drainage systems are installed. Trees or vines must then be planted and cared for, although they produce little or no income for about four to seven years, depending on the particular crop. Thereafter, crop income increases until trees or vines reach their prime production period after eight to ten years.

In spite of the long period from planting to maximum yield, there are benefits to be derived from such farming operations, such as:

☐ A significant portion of the property cost can be allocated to producing trees, vines and irrigation facilities that are depreciated over a five-year life under the ACRS rules. If the land is sold for residential or industrial development, the unrecovered grove and vine costs generally can be deducted against ordinary income as an abandonment loss. In that event, the profit is attributed only to the land and is normally realized as a capital gain.

☐ A cost allocation may be made to growing crops which may be offset against proceeds when harvested, or possibly deducted in the year of acquisition, if early enough in the crop cycle.

☐ The investment tax credit is available on the capitalized costs for the year in which the vineyard, orchard or grove comes into production.

☐ The underlying land value often reflects both inflation gains and increase in value due to population growth and the limited amount of available land that can be developed economically.

☐ Any gain realized on the sale of a vineyard, orchard or grove before depreciation commences qualifies for capital gain treatment in full, assuming the seller is not considered a dealer in land for tax purposes.

Horse Breeding and Racing

The thoroughbred and standardbred horse industries are multi-billion dollar businesses. Within the last several years, numerous limited partnerships have been formed to acquire, breed and race horses. These ventures have expanded opportunities for persons already in the horse industry by providing additional sources of capital. In addition, this investment technique has permitted newcomers to enter the industry at a significantly reduced cost.

Generally, the partnership operates as either a breeding or a racing partnership. A breeding partnership generally purchases broodmares, breeds them to specified stallions, and then sells the foals as weanlings or yearlings. The general partner receives a management fee for maintaining the horses and for determining the best stallion for each broodmare. Fees paid for the right to breed to a stallion are generally deductible when paid by a cash-basis taxpayer. Since the gestation period of a broodmare is 11 months, significant amounts of capital are required in the initial years.

Racing partnerships involve the purchase of race horses which are managed by a trainer, with a sharing of race proceeds and expenses. Hopefully, the racing record of the horse will increase its breeding value. This may result in a syndication (a sale of interests in the horse).

The tax benefits of horse operations involve the deferral of income — through the current deduction of depreciation, breeding fees and operating expenses — and the future realization of income, from racing, breeding and sale of the offspring. Also, there is the potential to realize long-term capital gain upon subsequent sale of the race or breeding horse for an amount greater than its cost if the horse is extremely successful.

Horses can generally be depreciated over five years. However, race horses over two years old and breeding horses over 12 years old have a three-year depreciable life. Horses are not eligible for the investment tax credit. Horses used for breeding or racing must be held for 24 months to be eligible for capital gain treatment.

The Risks of Farming

Investment in an agricultural tax shelter is not without substantial risk. Losses from disease, a poor birth rate, or a temporary drop in cattle prices, for example, can materially affect the economics of a cattle investment. An investor in tree crops, field crops and vineyards must carefully analyze a crop's potential production, prices, cost of maintenance, and overall risks. This evaluation includes an analysis of soil and weather conditions, the availability of water, the type and cost of energy required to produce the crop, the cost of acreage, the ability and cost to finance, the location and performance of the packing house through which the product will be harvested and sold, and the availability of competent, responsible management for ongoing operations. The investor is at the mercy of both domestic and world markets for farm commodities; for example, bumper crops can seriously weaken price structures. Labor sources and supply, and all their associated problems, also must be carefully considered. And national protectionist policies may serve to inhibit the free transfer of agricultural products among world markets.

Of substantial importance during the past decade has been the speculation in farm land and specialty permanent plantings (such as almonds and grapes) that has increased land prices beyond the levels recoverable through farming operations. Although tempered by the recent strength of the U.S. dollar, foreign investment in U.S. agricultural land has been a significant force in inflating land values. As a result, many existing investments are distressed and a "shake out" is currently taking place.

Chapter 8

Timber

ur forestlands are a vital part of the nation's economy. Approximately 500 million acres of land are devoted to the growth of commercial timber. Of that total, 28% is owned by the public through the federal government and other public agencies. Only 13% of our timberland is owned by integrated forest-products companies; 59% is owned by approximately four million private owners — individuals, farmers, partnerships, small corporations, etc. Together, these timberlands owners supply the basic raw material for a vast forest products industry whose many products, including lumber, paper and chemicals, touch the daily lives of all Americans.

Timber is unusual among our vital natural resources — it is renewable. The renewal of timber resources, however, is not automatic; timberlands require sustained-yield management to replenish them through reforestation, to protect them from natural disasters, and to harvest them with the least harm to the environment.

The growth of timber is a long and expensive undertaking. In no other business is the period from initial investment and ultimate realization so extended. Depending on the type of tree, the area in which it is planted and other factors, the planting of a seedling and its ultimate harvest as commercial timber may require from 25 to 75 years. During that time, the trees must be cultivated and protected from loss from fire, disease, storms and other natural disasters. During that time, too, the forests generate little or no income and the capital invested in them is fixed.

Because government recognizes the vital role that our forests fulfill in our economy, it has attempted to encourage long-term timber investments in spite of the natural and economic risks that such investments entail. One of the means chosen to encourage the regeneration of our timberlands is the tax law, which provides tax incentives for those who grow and harvest timber.

What Is Timber?

"Timber" may be narrowly perceived as applying only to trees usable for lumber, but its tax meaning also includes trees used for pulpwood, veneer, poles, pilings, crossties and other wood products. Nursery stock and Christmas trees do not qualify as timber, except those Christmas trees that are in excess of six years old at the time they are cut.

Tax Incentives

Although the forest-products industry may use various tax incentives generally available to any taxpayer, the industry, including private investors in timberlands, enjoys several tax incentives associated directly with the growth and harvesting of timber. These tax incentives are:

☐ Special capital gain treatment.

☐ Current deduction of certain costs.

☐ Special treatment of losses.

Capital Gain

Like many assets, timberlands and timber could qualify for capital gain treatment under long-standing provisions of the tax law, which confer such treatment on gains realized from the sale of capital assets and on real property used in a trade or business. To receive such favored treatment, however, requires strict conformity with the requirements of tax provisions that may be difficult to meet. Moreover, certain timber transactions, such as cutting for use in the owner's manufacturing operations, cannot meet the *sale or exchange* requirement of the usual capital gain transaction. Absent special consideration in the tax law, timber values that accumulate over a long and costly growth cycle of 25, 50, or even 75 years might ultimately be realized as ordinary income.

Because such prospects offered no inducement to timber investment, Congress long ago enacted tax provisions that confer capital gain treatment on timber transactions that otherwise might not qualify for such results. One provision allows the cutting of timber to be treated as a sale or exchange; the other confers capital gain treatment on disposals of timber with a retained economic interest.

Cutting of timber. Standing timber may be owned by the owner of the land on which it stands or by another who has the contractual right to cut it. In either case, the timber may be cut for sale to another or for use in the owner's trade or business. If the owner of such standing timber so *elects*, the cutting of the timber is considered a sale or exchange of the timber that qualifies for long-term capital gain treatment for tax purposes. To so qualify, the normal holding-period requirement of more than six months must be met. The election must be made in the taxpayer's timely filed return for the year in which the timber is cut and, once made, binds the taxpayer to the same tax treatment of timber cut in subsequent years.

The capital gain recognized on the cutting of timber is measured by the difference between the fair market value of the timber on the first day of the taxable year in which it was cut and the taxpayer's tax basis in the timber (technically referred to as the adjusted basis for depletion — see the following section on depletion). After cutting, that fair market value becomes the tax basis of the cut timber for all further taxable transactions. Any realization of amounts in excess of the fair market value when cut will be treated as ordinary income. Thus, gains and losses so realized — from changes in market values after the timber is cut, or from conversion of the timber into lumber or other products — yield ordinary income or loss.

Retained economic interest. Standing timber may be disposed of in certain transactions in which the timber owner retains an economic interest in the timber. In such instances, the timber owner surrenders the right to cut the timber in return for the right to share in the proceeds from its sale; any recovery of the owner's investment in the timber is thus conditioned upon the timber actually being severed from the land. A typical example of such a transaction is one in which the timber is sold on the stump, cut by the buyers, measured after cut, and paid for on a per unit-cut basis. Without some special provision in tax the law, such transactions would result in the realization of ordinary income.

At the time Congress enacted the relief provision granting capital gain treatment to the cutting of timber, it also extended such treatment to those transactions in which a timber owner (or any person who owns an interest in timber, including a sublessor or a holder of a contract to cut timber) disposed of timber and retained an economic interest therein. To qualify for such treatment, the normal holding-period requirement of more than six months must be met prior to cutting. Although it is essential that the payments received by the timber owner be based solely on the quantity of timber cut, the amount of these payments may be determined by various measures. In each case, however, the proceeds realized by the owner must result from the retention of an economic interest in the timber disposed of.

About depletion. Timber depletion is generally a misunderstood concept. This is especially true among persons outside the timber industry who equate timber depletion with the percentage depletion allowance for oil, gas and other natural resources.

As timber is cut, the owner is allowed to deduct the tax basis in the timber in determining gain or loss for tax purposes. This recovery of basis is referred to as cost depletion. An owner's tax basis in timber is generally the amount paid for the timber or the cutting rights plus any capital additions, and is technically referred to as the *adjusted basis for depletion*. Thus, if the owner elects capital gain treatment for the cutting of the timber, the so-called depletion deduction serves to reduce timber capital gain income. Unlike percentage depletion — which is measured by a percentage of gross income and which continues as long as the property produces revenue — timber depletion is measured by the quantity of timber that is cut and is limited to recovery of cost.

Current Deductions

Unlike the special relief provisions for the tax treatment of transactions involving the cutting or disposal of timber, there are no special rules in the law relating to expenditures to acquire, improve, manage or operate timber properties. Income tax regulations, however, require that costs incurred in the planting of timber must be capitalized and recovered through depletion. This treatment is consistent with tax rules that generally require capitalization of amounts expended for permanent improvements that increase the value of property.

Many of the costs incurred in growing timber are currently deductible for tax purposes as ordinary and necessary business expenses. Thus, once timber has been planted or otherwise acquired, the costs of cruising (estimating the quantity of uncut timber), thinning, brush control, pruning, salaries, and other costs of timber management are deductible. Interest on timberlands held solely as an investment, however, may be subject to the investment interest rules (see page 21).

The raising of timber can also result in current deductions by virtue of special exclusions from tax provisions that otherwise limit these deductions when incurred. Thus, timber is excluded from the provisions that prohibit current deductions for prepaid farm supplies, and from those that require the capitalization of preproductive period costs for citrus groves and orchards. However, timber may be subject to the premature accrual rules (see page 27).

Losses

Timber transactions involving the cutting of timber and the disposal of timber in which an economic interest has been retained can result in losses as well as gains. In such case, the relief provisions previously discussed that allow capital gain treatment for gains operate to allow special treatment of losses. Such losses are considered to be losses sustained on the sale of assets used in a trade or business; if the total of all such losses exceeds the gains realized on the sale of business assets, that excess is treated as an ordinary loss for tax purposes. However, gains from the sale of timber are recharacterized as ordinary income if there was a net loss from the sale of business assets during the previous five years. In a partnership setting, each partner must separately account for the distributive share of the partnership's gains or losses on the sale of business assets; thus, each partner must also apply this five-year "lookback" rule on an individual basis. This "lookback" provision is effective for tax years beginning after 1984.

Alternative Minimum Tax

Long-term capital gains realized by individuals from timber transactions are tax preference items subject to the AMT (see pages 23 and 25). Like all such preference items that arise from shelter investing, timber capital gains need to be taken into account in an investor's tax planning in order to minimize the impact of the AMT.

Timber as an Investment

Although the ownership of timber offers opportunities for the realization of capital gain, it generally is not as favored by tax shelter investors as are other investments. This lack of preference can be ascribed to several factors, such as:

☐ Timber offers few front-end tax deductions in the year of acquisition.

☐ Timber requires a substantial, long-term investment of funds.

☐ Timber requires incurring significant carrying costs during a non-productive period in which no income is realized.

☐ Timber as an investment is unfamiliar to most investors.

☐ Timber generally has not been "packaged" and sold by tax shelter promoters.

Investors considering timber as an investment must evaluate it not only against those factors that apply to all investments but also those that are peculiar to timber.

Investment Considerations

Timber is raised in various parts of the country, thus, a timber investor must first decide on the location of the investment. In doing so, the investor must consider the quality, kind and growth rate of timber in one area as compared with other growth areas. These factors are governed by soil, water and weather conditions, and the elevation and location of land. The investor should also consider the requirements that timber be accessible, so it can be economically cut and transported to market. A prospective investor ordinarily should consult professional foresters before deciding where to make a timber investment.

An investor should also consider the probable effect of environmental issues on the growth and harvesting of the timber, and the projected impact of local property tax structures on future carrying costs.

The extraordinary risks of timber ownership must also be considered. Severe losses can be suffered from disease, fire, windstorms, tornadoes, hurricanes, earthquakes, volcano eruptions, etc. Insurance generally cannot be secured to protect against such disasters.

An investor must also consider that the demand for timber is cyclical and is heavily dependent on the health of the construction (particularly the housing) industry.

Management of timber properties may also be a problem for most investors, as it is in any case of absentee ownership. Consulting foresters, however, generally can be retained to perform forest management services for a fee.

Financing Timber

Manufacturers often find it desirable to own or control a guaranteed source of raw materials, and this is no less true in the forest-products industry. Unlike other industries, however, timber requires costly reforestation programs and considerable time to develop to mature stands. Forest products companies need to acquire additional supplies of raw materials, coupled with high capital costs, has resulted in the development of new methods of financing the acquisition of timberlands. Thus, combinations of contracts — such as cutting contracts, production payments, and long-term leases — have been used in cooperative arrangements involving forest products companies, investor groups, and investment bankers.

Under one such arrangement, a joint venture with the forest products company is formed to acquire existing timberlands subject to long-term, take-or-pay cutting contracts. The investment banking group arranges the financing, with the property and the long-term cutting contract as security. The long-term contract requires a minimum annual payment sufficient to fund all carrying costs and to provide a reasonable return to the investors. If the transaction is properly structured, the joint venture owners might retain the tax incentives of reporting capital gain on payments received under the cutting contract, and current deduction of interest and other carrying costs. Investors often receive all or part of the residuals available at the end of the contract term.

Under these arrangements, the timber producer may obtain capital gain treatment from subsequent harvesting of the timber while obtaining control of and financing for the needed timberland.

Absentee investor participation in the ownership of timber properties is likely to increase both as forest products companies require additional financing sources and as investor understanding of the timber industry increases.

Motion Pictures

The credibility of motion pictures as a tax shelter investment has been shaken by various questionable offerings that have attracted the displeasure of the Internal Revenue Service. The extremely high cost of producing and distributing such films, however, still makes it necessary for major studios and independent producers to seek significant amounts of financing from private investors. Properly structured, such investments are a legitimate form of tax shelter for high-bracket investors who have critically weighed and accepted the risks inherent in the film industry.

The Risks

The greatest risk involved in a motion picture is the risk of "box office" failure. A film without an audience may or may not be a critical failure; clearly, it is a financial failure.

Although films entail the assumption of tax risks that are normally present in any tax shelter investment, they must also entail the assumption of substantial economic risk if they are to achieve the tax benefits sought by the investor. Such risks can no longer be hedged through nonrecourse financing, for tax deductions and credits can be gained only if an investor is at risk on the investment.

Tax Considerations

Motion picture tax shelters were one of the targets of tax reform exemplified by the adoption of the at-risk rules. Certain provisions of that legislation significantly altered the income tax treatment of these shelter investments.

Depreciation

The owner of an interest in a motion picture is entitled to depreciate the *pro rata* share of the capital costs of production or acquisition. However, films and videotapes are not recovery property and therefore must be depreciated using a method which is not expressed in years. Depreciation is first available in the year in which the film is ready and available for public exhibition. The depreciable basis of a film must be adjusted for the investment credit claimed. These rules make the election to reduce the investment credit in lieu of a basis adjustment (see page 18) inapplicable to films.

The usual method of depreciation for films is the income-forecast method, which generally produces an accelerated writeoff of costs. Under this method, the amount of the depreciation deduction is computed by multiplying the capitalized cost of the motion picture by a fraction; the numerator is the net receipts from the film for the taxable year (such receipts normally are greatest in the first year), and the denominator is the estimated total receipts from the film over its life.

Investment Credit

Motion pictures qualify for investment tax credit equal to 6⅔% of "qualified U.S.production costs." The credit is available in the year the film is released.

If at least 80% of a film's direct production costs are incurred in the United States, investment credit will be allowed on all U.S. production costs, including labor, overhead, and screen rights. If less than 80% of a film's direct costs are incurred in the United States, the credit will be allowed only on direct U.S. production costs, excluding overhead, screen rights, and foreign production costs.

Films depreciated under the income-forecast method may also yield a full 10% investment credit, but at the cost of recognizing recapture of the credit upon disposition of the film or recovery of 90% of its cost through depreciation. Otherwise, recapture can be avoided, while using the income-forecast method, by claiming the lesser credit of 6⅔%.

Investment credit is allowable to a taxpayer only to the extent of the taxpayer's ownership interest in the motion picture at the time of its initial release. A person's ownership interest is determined on the basis of the *pro rata* share of any loss which may be incurred on the production costs of the film. This test is similar to the at-risk limitation imposed on the deductibility of losses. However, it extends to all taxpayers, not just to individuals and certain closely held corporations.

Typical Motion Picture Tax Shelters

The two most common types of motion picture tax shelters are the "negative pickup" partnership and the "advertising-service" partnership.

Negative Pickup Partnership

Under the negative pickup arrangement, a partnership is formed to purchase a completed or partially completed motion picture from an independent producer or a major studio (the producer) for distribution through a major studio or an independent distribution operation. The partnership normally gives the producer a down payment and issues a promissory note for the balance. Typically, the producer is also given a profit participation in the film. It was common practice prior to the adoption of the at-risk rules to have all or a portion of the promissory note payable solely from the profits of the film. Another formerly frequent arrangement specified that the promissory note was to be converted from recourse to nonrecourse upon attaining a certain level of gross receipts. Losses arising under such arrangements are now denied under the at-risk rules (see page 22).

Leveraged purchasing enables the partnership to claim depreciation and investment credit on a cost basis that is substantially in excess of the cash investment of the partners. An investor must be cautious in entering into these arrangements, since the at-risk rules must be complied with to gain deductions and credits. An investor should also consider that the basis for determining the investment credit is the qualified U.S. production costs, not the purchase price of the film.

Advertising Service Partnership

In the typical advertising service arrangement, a partnership purchases a completed motion picture and finances 100% of the cost with a recourse note. The investors become limited partners in exchange for cash contributions essentially equal to the advertising expenditures necessary to exploit the partnership's motion picture. The limited partners share in income, losses and credits in the same manner as in the negative pickup partnership. These investments are structured so that a deduction for advertising is taken in the first year, with the income generated in subsequent years. However, recent legislation may have an impact on this arrangement. Generally, no deductions are allowed for advertising costs until the services have been performed. (See page 27 for discussion of the economic performance rule.)

Other Motion Picture Tax Shelters

Other variations on the basic theme of motion picture tax shelters have been and still are being used. The following are among the more common types.

One type that was very popular prior to recent tax reforms was the production-service company. In the typical situation, the production-service company partnership would enter into a contract with the owner of the screen rights (usually a major motion picture company) to provide the services relating to the actual filming of the motion picture on behalf of the ultimate owner of the film. Taking the position that the partnership was engaged in a service business, the partnership would deduct in the year paid the cost of the services rendered pursuant to its contract with the owner of the screen rights. By deducting all the expenditures in the year incurred and receiving payment for the services in a subsequent year, a tax deduction of 4:1 often was claimed by the partners by virtue of nonrecourse financing. The at-risk rules eliminated any possibility for individual taxpayers to deduct these expenditures, although such deductions may be available to corporate partners that are neither S corporations nor personal holding companies.

Another arrangement that has become common is one in which major studios form partnerships, contribute story rights, and take on limited partners to share in the actual production costs of the motion picture. Once the film is produced, the partnership enters into a distribution agreement with the major studio. In this arrangement, the limited partners share in the entire production and distribution cycle, a marked difference from the operations of the negative pick-up partnership, in which the partners purchase a completed film for distribution. This method is also used by independent producers who lack sufficient capital to produce their films without outside financing.

Research and Development

lthough they offer a potential for significant returns to investors, research and development (R&D) tax shelters are perhaps the most unsung of all. That may reflect the risk normally associated with such programs, which is substantial, but it may also indicate the degree of their unfamiliarity to most investors. Their unfamiliarity, however, can be expected to decrease as more R&D ventures become available for the development of new products, such as computer technology.

Their Structure

Most R&D tax shelters are structured as limited partnerships, for the reasons discussed previously, such as flow-through of tax attributes to the limited partners, limited liability, etc. The general partner in such programs is normally a subsidiary of the corporation that wishes to undertake a specific research project but wants to fund the research costs from outside sources. The limited partners supply those funds through their participation in the R&D partnership.

In these arrangements, the R&D partnership typically does not itself conduct the research; that is actually done by the general partner under a development contract with the partnership. If the research efforts are successful, the resulting product or process is licensed to the parent of the general partner for sale or use; royalties are paid to the R&D partnership. Ultimately, the product or process may be sold to the general partner or to a third party.

R&D Defined

Research and development costs (or research and experimental expenditures, as they are termed in the tax law) are those expenditures:

> . . . incurred in connection with the taxpayer's trade or business which represent research and development costs in the experimental or laboratory sense. The term includes generally all such costs incident to the development of an experimental or pilot model, a plant process, a product, a formula, an invention, or similar property, and the improvement of already existing property of the type mentioned. . . .

What They Offer

Research and development tax shelters offer two significant rewards to investors: rapid write-off of costs and potential capital gain.

Congress has deemed it necessary to provide these incentives to encourage the development of new products and processes that will retain for our country a dominant position in the increasingly spirited, international race for technological advances.

Rapid Write-Off

When R&D efforts are successful, they result in the creation of an asset that may have value over a substantial period. Under general tax rules, the costs incurred to develop such an asset would be capitalized and recovered over the asset's useful life. When such costs represent R&D costs, however, the taxpayer has two liberal options which may be used to recover these costs:

☐ The costs may be expensed as they are incurred, (but no deduction is generally allowed for prepaid R&D costs), or

☐ The costs may be treated as deferred expenses and recovered over a period of not less than 60 months.

It is the first option on which R&D tax shelter partnerships are based.

Capital Gain Potential

If an R&D tax shelter partnership is successful in producing a marketable product or process, it ordinarily authorizes the use of that asset by others under a licensing arrangement that provides royalties to the partnership as compensation for that use. Favorable tax rules afford special treatment to such royalties received by inventors and individuals who have obtained an interest in the property by payment of money prior to the practical use of the product or process. In such case, as when an invention is sold, the payments received may qualify as long-term capital gain. To do so, however, the payments must apply to an asset that is patentable. Certain assets, such as computer software, may not be patentable; thus, their licensing may result in ordinary income. In some cases even non patentable assets may receive capital gain treatment if certain requirements, including requisite holding periods, are met.

The potential for realizing capital gain from successful R&D efforts is a significant factor in assessing the benefits an investor may gain from an R&D tax shelter partnership investment.

At-Risk Rules

Like most other tax shelters, R&D tax shelter programs are subject to the at-risk rules that limit their tax benefits from losses and investment credits to the amount of capital at risk, either from direct investment of the investor's funds or through debt for which the investor is personally liable.

Alternative Minimum Tax

The deduction arising from the election to expense R&D costs in the year incurred can subject an investor to the AMT (see page 23). The amount of the tax preference item arising from that deduction is the excess of the R&D deduction for the year over the amount that would have been allowed as a deduction had the R&D costs been capitalized and amortized ratably over 10 years. A taxpayer may avoid having R&D costs classified as an item of tax preference by electing to capitalize the costs and recover them ratably over 10 years.

The classification of R&D as an AMT preference item and the ability of a taxpayer to avoid having it so classified make it imperative that an investor incurring R&D costs carefully plan personal tax affairs in order to minimize the amount of tax due. The fact that the preference/no preference election is an annual one affords some flexibility in that planning.

Qualified Research Expenses

Certain "qualified research expenses" can yield a substantial tax credit. The credit is based on *incremental* R&D expenditures and is allowed at a rate of 25% on the excess of:

□ The qualified research expenses for the year, over

□ The base period research expenses (average of three prior years).

Unfortunately, this credit appears to be unavailable to investors in the usual R&D tax shelter partnership. The reason is the stringent "trade-or-business" requirement that must be met to qualify for the credit.

Tax rules sometimes make distinctions that may appear to be overly subtle. Distinguishing between a cost that is incurred "in connection with a trade or business" and one that is incurred "in carrying on a trade or business" is one of those subtleties. To qualify for the option to deduct R&D costs (see page 102) requires the less stringent "in connection with" standard; to qualify for the R&D credit requires the more demanding "in carrying on" test.

It is not necessary to belabor these distinctions here; it is necessary, however, to say that Congress intended the R&D credit to be available only in those cases where the expenditures were incurred in a particular trade or business that was being carried on at the time the costs were incurred. Thus, it was not the lawmaker's intent to allow the credit for R&D costs that relate to a *potential* trade or business (not being carried on at the time the costs were incurred). This effectively denies the credit to a new entity which undertakes research with the intention of exploiting the results through future production and sales; it also effectively denies the credit to an existing business that incurs R&D in order to enter a new trade or business.

The "in-carrying-on" requirement for earning the R&D credit makes the credit unavailable for expenditures for outside or contract research intended to be transferred to another in return for license or royalty payments. Thus, the credit was apparently not intended to be available to new organizations, such as R&D tax shelter partnerships, whose purpose is to sell or finance the technology arising from the research.

Because of the narrow "trade-or-business" requirements of the R&D credit, it is improbable that the activities of the usual R&D tax shelter partnership can be structured to qualify for this credit.

Securities, Commodities and Other Investments

lthough stocks and bonds have been the classic means of raising capital, they generally have not been considered prime vehicles for tax shelter investing. The principal reason for this is that such securities ordinarily do not offer substantial first-year losses, like oil and gas investments, or losses that may exceed the initial cash investment, like real estate. They do, however, offer other attributes of tax shelter investments, such as the potential for gain taxed at favorable rates; indeed, some offer income that is entirely exempt from federal taxation. Accordingly, stocks and bonds should also be considered for investment by a tax shelter investor.

Securities and Commodities Transactions

Short sales, puts and calls (including listed options) and certain straddles, in both securities and commodities, are techniques that may be used to achieve certain tax objectives. Because of their technical nature, however, investment advisers, brokers and dealers should be consulted by a prospective investor in order to minimize the risks inherent in such investments by ensuring that the techniques used will yield the desired results.

Locking in Gain With a Short Sale

A short sale against-the-box can be used to lock in economic gain (but it forfeits the chance for further gain) while deferring the gain's recognition for tax purposes to a subsequent year. This affords an investor who owns substantially appreciated securities an excellent opportunity for tax planning. The investor can either sell the securities and immediately recognize taxable income or sell the securities short at substantially the same price and defer the recognition of taxable income until settlement of the short sale. The interim period until settlement does not change the holding period of the security, since the holding period is suspended on the date of the short sale. Therefore, if a security sold short has not been held for over six months at the time of the sale, short-term capital gain results when the short sale is covered.

Converting a Capital Loss Into an Ordinary Loss

An investor who has capital losses that cannot be used currently may use a short sale to effectively convert those losses to ordinary losses that currently reduce taxable income. This can be accomplished through the short sale of borrowed stock. When stock is sold short just prior to its ex-dividend date, the dividend received by the borrower must be repaid to the lender of the stock. This repayment represents an ordinary deduction for tax purposes if the short sale is held open and the risk of loss is not limited by an offsetting position for at least 46 days. If the price of the stock declines subsequent to the ex-dividend date in an amount that is substantially equivalent to the dividend payout, then covering the short sale results in a short-term capital gain approximately equal to the dividend repayment. This gain is offset by the investor's capital losses that otherwise could not have been used. However, if the short sale is not held open for at least 46 days, the dividend repayment is not deductible for tax purposes. Instead, the dividend repayment is added to the seller's basis in the stock used to close the short sale. This reduces any gain, or increases any loss, on the sale instead of producing a deduction.

Brokers / Dealers

Brokers/dealers in securities, options, physical commodities, etc. may be able to manage their portfolios of inventory and investments to achieve deferrals of ordinary income, possibly converting such income to capital gain. Some brokers/dealers are organized as limited partnerships and can pass on these advantageous tax consequences to the limited partners.

The brokers/dealers' ordinary losses allocated to limited partners may be limited to income from a similar trade or business carried on by the limited partner. Any disallowed loss can be carried forward until it can be used against the related trade-or-business income. There are exceptions, however, to this rule for economic losses.

Section 1256 Contracts

The over-six-months holding period (12 months for securities purchased before June 23, 1984) requirement for long-term capital gains does not apply to certain securities defined as Section 1256 Contracts (contracts). Regardless of their holding period, gains and losses in contracts are considered to be 60% long-term and 40% short-term. Moreover, gains and losses on contracts are recognized for tax purposes on a "mark-to-market" basis, either on taking delivery of the property underlying the contracts or at yearend, whether or not gain or loss has actually been realized through disposition of the contract.

Need for Counseling

As the above discussion indicates, there are numerous security investments available in the financial marketplace. Each of those, however, has different economic and tax attributes. It is important that these be carefully evaluated to determine if the results they produce for a particular investor are the ones desired. Possible erosion of investment capital by inflation must be considered also in connection with any long-term investment in fixed-obligation securities. Because of the technical complexities of many securities transactions, competent investment counseling is mandatory.

Corporate Bonds and Certain U.S. Government Obligations

Bonds issued when interest rates were substantially lower than current rates sell at a discount. Discount bonds (both corporate and long-term U.S. government obligations) offer the investor not only an opportunity to achieve a significant yield but also the opportunity to defer the tax on this income. Interest income from U.S. government obligations offers the added advantage of exemption from state taxation. These bonds can be purchased with little equity (sometimes as little as 5% or 10%), with the balance of the purchase price financed through borrowing. The interest payable on the debt thus incurred is deductible (subject to the investment interest limitation; see page 21 and page 22). The interest that is earned in the form of amortization of the discount on the bond is not taxed until the bond matures or is sold, unless the investor elects to currently recognize the market discount amortization (see page 108). For bonds issued before July 18, 1984, appreciation becomes long-term capital gain at the time of the sale, providing the bond has been held over 12 months (six months if purchased after June 23, 1984). For bonds issued on July 18, 1984, or later, the market discount portion of the appreciation becomes ordinary income and any excess becomes long-term capital gain if the bond has been held over six months. See the discussion of market discount (page 108) for computational rules.

As with all tax incentives, it is also necessary to consider the nontax economics of such investments (safety, liquidity, yield, alternative investments, etc.) and the possible effect of the alternative minimum tax on long-term capital gains (see page 23). An investor also must be able to demonstrate that this tax planning technique involves an assumption of economic risk and a potential for economic gain beyond its tax benefits.

In assessing the relative merits of different bond issues, an investor should seek the counsel of an investment adviser. In determining which issue is best suited to personal needs, an investor must consider the current income yield from the bond coupons and the bond maturities. The income derived from the current coupon can be used to offset, to some degree, the current interest expense incurred to carry the bonds.

Financing

Like other investments, the acquisition of bonds can be financed in various ways. One means that should not be overlooked by the individual investor is borrowing the required funds on the cash surrender value of a life insurance policy. This type of loan generally is available at a very favorable interest rate. Alternatively, an arrangement may be made with a bank to finance the purchase of bonds by use of a renewable note. The principal disadvantage of this arrangement is the unpredictability of the interest rate and the chance that the bank may decline to renew the note. Such nonrenewal could force an investor to liquidate a position at a time when the investor would realize a loss. The investment interest limitation (see page 21), the net interest limitation rules relating to market discount bonds and short-term obligations, and special limitations on deducting interest on life insurance loans must also be considered in these financing arrangements.

Interest Rate Changes

Changes in interest rates can have a significant effect on the value of bond investments. A substantial decrease in current interest rates generally causes the value of bonds to increase to a level that properly reflects the effect of current rates on bond yields. When this occurs, an investor may be able to realize currently long-term gains (assuming that it is not a market discount bond or an OID instrument) that would otherwise have been obtained only on maturity of the bonds. Conversely, a significant increase in current interest rates generally will cause the value of bonds to fall. This can create capital losses that perhaps can be overcome only by holding the bonds to maturity. In cases where the investor is unable to hold such bonds until maturity, losses may be realized at a time when they do not fit into the investor's overall tax planning strategies.

Original issue discount. The tax consequences discussed above may not apply to certain bonds that were originally issued at a discount. Such original issue discount (OID) existing at the date of purchase of certain corporate bonds is taxed currently as ordinary income. This discount must be reported for income tax purposes on a yield-to-maturity basis over the life of the bonds, even though this income is not matched by current cash receipts. For this reason, some investors may prefer to limit purchases of bonds to those issued at par. Others must take this factor into account in the determination of net yield from their bond investments. An investor's broker ordinarily should be able to identify which bonds are subject to the OID rules.

Market discount bonds. As interest rates rise, the market value of a bond may fall below its maturity value, giving rise to market discount. For most bonds, this discount (when realized) is treated as a capital gain. For obligations issued after July 18, 1984, however, taxpayers are required to determine the amount of market discount on the day the bond is purchased and treat such discount as interest income spread evenly over the period from purchase to maturity. The taxpayer may elect to accrue the discount each year, or treat the cumulative discount amortization as interest when the bond is sold. Appreciation in excess of the market discount becomes capital gain when the bond is sold. Depreciation subsequent to the purchase of the bond is a capital loss when the bond is sold.

If a market discount bond is leveraged, the interest expense is allowed as a deduction only to the extent it exceeds the amount of market discount. Upon disposition of the market discount bond, the previously disallowed interest expense is deductible.

Zero-Coupon Bonds

Corporate borrowers sometimes issue low-interest rate or so-called zero-coupon bonds. These bonds offer significant cash flow advantages to the borrower, since they require little or no current cash outlay to service the debt. The interest is paid substantially or wholly at maturity through redemption of the bonds at par. An additional reason for the popularity of these bonds in recent years was the method the borrower was allowed to use in determining the interest deduction for tax purposes. The discount was recognized ratably over the life of the bond. Since this method does not recognize the compounding element inherent in such transactions, interest deductions were accelerated for tax purposes. Under current law, this compounding must be recognized for bonds issued after July 1, 1982; the result is that interest deductions are redistributed, with decreased deductions in early years and increased deductions in later years. This change may decrease the use of zero-coupon bonds in the future.

The investor in such low-interest or zero coupon bonds must include a portion of the OID in taxable income each year, even though no cash is received. In the past, the amount included was a ratable portion of the discount. For bonds issued after July 1, 1982, the amount recognized is determined in the same manner as is the interest deduction of the borrower. Compared to ratable recognition, this decreases the income recognized in earlier years and increases it for later years.

Some investors may not be concerned by this requirement to report taxable income without cash flow, perhaps because they are offsetting it with other tax shelter losses or because they are tax-exempt organizations such as pension funds, Keogh plans or IRAs. Investment in such bonds can be very attractive to those investors, since they do offer a long-term guaranteed rate of return on both the original funds invested and the reinvested interest.

Treasury Bills

U.S. Treasury bills carry no coupons and are always sold at a discount from face value to reflect current interest rates. This discount — the difference between the price paid for the instrument and its face value — represents ordinary income and is amortized ratably over the remaining life of the bill. For some taxpayers, such as accrual-basis taxpayers, income is recognized over the life of the Treasury bill on a ratable basis. Any gain recognized in excess of the ratable amortization of the discount represents short-term capital gain. Conversely, any loss realized on disposition of the bill is short-term capital loss.

For cash-basis taxpayers, the income from a Treasury bill is not taxable until maturity. If the bill is leveraged, however, a cash-basis taxpayer must defer the interest expense equal to the amortized discount until the bill reaches maturity or is sold. An election can be made by a cash-basis taxpayer to pick up the income currently and avoid the interest deferral.

Municipal Bonds

Tax-exempt bonds (commonly called municipal bonds) are those issued by states, cities, other political subdivisions, and certain public authorities. Investments in municipal bonds ordinarily result in the following advantages to an investor:

☐ Exemption of interest from federal taxation.

☐ Exemption of interest from state taxation in the state of issuance.

☐ Wide selection of maturity dates.

☐ Security.

☐ Liquidity (marketability).

☐ Attractive yields.

Financing Through Debt

There are also several adverse factors related to municipal bond investments that should be considered by an investor before investing in such issues. For example, an investor cannot leverage an investment position in tax-exempt securities by borrowing part of the purchase price and still obtain a tax deduction for the interest paid on such borrowing. Federal tax law specifically disallows a deduction for interest on indebtedness incurred or continued to purchase or carry tax-exempt obligations. A taxpayer who purchases or holds tax-exempt securities through investment of personal funds — but has other debt outstanding — may run the risk of having the interest on that other debt disallowed as a deduction under the theory that it is actually interest on indebtedness incurred or continued to purchase or carry the tax-exempt obligations. In support of that position, it could be argued that the tax-exempt securities could have been sold and the other debt liquidated.

Capital Gain Potential

Tax-exempt obligations bearing a low coupon rate issued at par value years ago may be selling at a substantial discount in relation to par value today. This market discount offers significant opportunities for the realization of capital gain if the obligations are held to maturity. This fact, of course, is taken into consideration in the market prices at which such bonds are sold. Very few municipal bonds are issued *originally* at a discount. To the extent that they are, this OID is amortized into income, using the constant-interest method, as exempt interest on which no tax is payable. The basis of the obligation is increased by the amount of this accrued tax-exempt OID. For obligations issued after September 3, 1982, and acquired after March 1, 1984, capital gain is limited to the gain in excess of the accrued tax-exempt OID.

Mortgage-Subsidy Bonds

Mortgage-subsidy bonds are a form of municipal bond that has been used to raise funds to provide residential mortgage financing at favorable rates. Their history has been somewhat controversial, and the interest earned on such bonds issued after 1987 will not qualify for tax exemption.

Return and Risk

The net return on municipal bonds should be measured on an after-tax basis to compare the return with that which could be realized from taxable bonds. For example, an individual in a 40% marginal tax bracket would require a 16⅔% return on a taxable investment to equal the yield on a 10% taxfree bond. The higher the tax rate, the more attractive is the yield on the municipal bond.

There are many types of municipal bonds, varying from general-obligation bonds, secured by the full taxing power of the issuer, to authority bonds, payable only from the net revenues of a special project such as a turnpike or a stadium. Since these different types of bonds entail varying degrees of risk, an investor must carefully select the degree of risk to be assumed.

Certain mutual funds can pass tax-exempt interest through to their shareholders. This device may offer an opportunity for an investor to spread the risk among various issues to an extent not possible by direct investment in municipals.

Industrial Development Bonds

A type of tax-exempt bond used frequently by businesses to raise capital is the industrial development bond (IDB). The IDB is designed to assist state and local governments in their efforts to attract private business to stimulate development of selected areas through increased employment and related benefits.

Why They Are Used

Although the major significance of IDBs for individual investors is their status as tax-exempt obligations, it may be helpful to investors to know why such bonds are so widely used.

The IDB can be an attractive vehicle for financing plant expansion or even for the acquisition of an existing building for rehabilitation. Because of its tax-exempt status, the IDB may carry an interest rate significantly below that required for taxable bonds. It can be a valuable financing tool not only for the smaller company for which other methods of financing may be unavailable, but also for a larger company as a supplement to customary methods of financing.

Typically, an IDB is issued by a state or local government authority that uses the proceeds to build an industrial plant for lease or sale to an industrial corporation. The formal arrangement between the corporation and the government unit that issues the IDB is generally structured as a lease or installment sale of the facilities, with sufficient payments being made by the company to cover interest and principal of the IDB. Title to the property generally passes to the company when the IDB is retired. The issuer of the IDB is ordinarily protected from liability if the corporation defaults on the agreement. For tax and financial reporting purposes, the IDB arrangement is a financing transaction; accordingly, the cost of the facilities and the related debt are treated by the company as if it owned the facilities and issued the IDB. There are numerous technical requirements for IDBs to be tax-exempt, but an investor usually is given some protection from the adverse tax consequences that could result from failure to meet such exemption requirements. In almost every case, an IDB issue is covered by an agreement that partially protects an investor's tax posture by requiring that the interest rate be increased if the IDB is determined not to be tax exempt.

Return on Investment

Acritical part of the evaluation of a tax shelter investment is the assessment of its risk and its potential reward. The assessment of risk is ultimately a subjective evaluation, although it may be based on certain factual information. The measurement of potential reward is a more objective exercise, although it must deal with factors that are largely unknowns. For example, the amounts and timing of cash flow are only estimates or projections, not guarantees. The subjective risk evaluation also affects the assessment of reward, for the risk in an investment must be considered in determining the return on investment that is acceptable to the investor in light of the risk.

One of the principal shortcomings of many tax shelter investors is their failure to logically and consistently measure the potential return on investment (ROI) in tax shelter transactions. A possible explanation for this lack is that there are *many* ways of measuring ROI and no clearly *best* way. Even so, this explanation should not preclude the use of the various alternatives that are available for measuring ROI. An investor should choose the method that best reflects the investor's own idea of how return should be measured, the chosen method needs to be applied consistently. In fact, an investor may choose to use more than one method in the ROI determination, seeking to support the results of one approach with the findings of another.

It is difficult to discuss ROI without getting bogged down in mathematical computations. Because such detail may only serve to intimidate or to aggravate some readers (and perhaps evoke memories of the "multiplication is vexation" rhyme quoted in Chapter 1), this chapter treats ROI in conceptual terms, with a minimum of mathematics.

As was noted earlier, there is no *one* preferred way to compute ROI. There are, however, several commonly used methods, each doubtless associated with a host of variations or refinements. The purpose of this discussion of ROI is simply to make the investor aware of several alternatives available for investment analysis, not to school the investor in their application. However, a general knowledge of those methods should enable an investor considering a sizable shelter investment opportunity to discuss it more knowledgeably with tax and investment advisers.

Payback Method

One way to view an investment is to consider how long it will take to recoup it, after which time any further return represents gain. When annual cash flow is constant, this is a matter of simple arithmetic — you divide the amount of the original net investment by the anticipated annual cash flow (including income taxes saved). The result represents the number of years that are required to recoup the original net investment, but it ignores future potential gains, cash flow and tax liability.

When annual cash flow is not uniform, this method still may be used to determine when payback occurs. In that case, the anticipated after-tax cash flows are accumulated to determine the year in which the original investment is recovered.

Although the payback method of analysis may be valid for some purposes, it has serious weaknesses that make it impractical as a tool for tax shelter investment analysis. In addition to its failure to look beyond payback, it does not recognize differences in cash-flow timing. For example, two different investments made at the same time may achieve payback in the same year. But they are not necessarily equal, since one may generate greater cash flow in the early years of the investment than does the other.

Another limitation of the payback method is that it doesn't really tell an investor anything about the rate of return on the investment; usually, it is the rate of return — how effectively the invested capital works — that interests most investors.

Cash-on-Cash

Measuring ROI in terms of cash return on cash investment is a simple method that is used by some investors. In that method, the annual return is divided by the amount invested without any adjustment to the numerator and denominator for the impact of taxes on those factors. Some experienced investors, particularly those in real estate, like the simplicity of this cash-on-cash measurement and apparently use it effectively to assure themselves of an investment's pre-tax economic viability. It is best left to those investors, however, since it is not a method that yields a completely meaningful result for most shelter investors.

Present Value

The key element lacking in the two investment analysis methods previously discussed is the ability to measure *future returns* in terms of *today's value*. This is a serious failing, since the value of money is affected by its timing; that is, by when it will be received. The basic operation of the time value of money can be readily demonstrated by example: Anyone would prefer to have a dollar today than to have the same dollar a year from today. A dollar today is simply worth more than a dollar that will not be received until some time in the future. The value of the future dollar is diminished both because of the probable effect of inflation and because it cannot earn a return until it is actually received.

By use of standard discount or present value tables (provided in Appendix F), anyone can determine the present value of a dollar amount that will be received at some definite time in the future. To make this determination, however, an acceptable discount rate must first be selected. For example, an investor who seeks a 10% rate of return on an investment would use a 10% discount rate to determine that $1,000 to be paid five years from today is worth only $621 today. Thus, $621 is the amount that the investor would have to invest today at 10%, compounded annually, to have $1,000 five years from today.

A tax shelter investor can use this basic discounting or present value method to assess the desirability of a particular investment as measured against alternative investments. For example, assume that an investor is offered an investment that promises to yield the following flow of cash. Each amount shown has been increased by its tax benefits or reduced by its tax detriments; that is, the amounts are *after* taxes. It is assumed that all transactions occur on the last day of the year.

After-Tax Investor's Cash Flow

Original investment —	1985	$(10,000)
Cash flow after taxes —	1986	4,000
	1987	2,000
	1988	1,000
	1989	3,000
	1990	5,000
Net cash flow		$ 5,000

Assuming the investor must have an 8% after-tax return on the investment, the future after-tax cash flow can be valued as follows:

Present Value Computations — 8%

Year of Receipt	Cash Flow Amount	Present Value Factor	Present Value Amount
1986	$ 4,000	.9259	$ 3,704
1987	2,000	.8573	1,715
1988	1,000	.7938	794
1989	3,000	.7350	2,205
1990	5,000	.6806	3,403
	$15,000		$11,821

These computations show that the present value of the future cash flows ($11,821) exceeds the amount of the investment ($10,000) by $1,821. This difference is known as the *net present value*.

When the net present value of an investment is a positive amount (as in the above example), an investor knows that the investment promises a return that exceeds the rate required for that investment. Conversely, when the net present value is a negative amount, the investor knows that its promised return falls short of the required rate. When the net present value is zero, the proposed investment promises a yield that is exactly the rate of return by which the investor has chosen to measure its potential.

Internal Rate of Return

In the example just discussed, the investor can readily see that the investment return exceeds the 8% after-tax return that was required. The investor does not, however, know the rate of return actually earned on the investment. That rate is obviously worth knowing, but how is it determined? The internal rate of return analysis is designed to answer that question.

The internal rate of return (IRR) of an investment is simply the rate that will discount future cash flows to an amount that equals the amount invested; thus, the IRR results in a net present value of zero. Using the same facts as in the preceding example, an after-tax IRR of 14.38% is the result. This can be demonstrated as follows:

Present Value Computations — 14.38%

Year of Receipt	Cash Flow Amount	Present Value Factor	Present Value Amount
1986	$ 4,000	.8743	$ 3,497
1987	2,000	.7644	1,528
1988	1,000	.6683	668
1989	3,000	.5843	1,753
1990	5,000	.5108	2,554
	$15,000		$10,000

The fact that the amount invested earns 14.38% while it remains invested can be proved by the following analysis.

Analysis of Cash Flows

Year	Beginning Amount Invested	14.38% Return	Cash Receipts	Ending Amount Invested
1986	$10,000	$1,438	$ (4,000)	$7,438
1987	7,438	1,070	(2,000)	6,508
1988	6,508	936	(1,000)	6,444
1989	6,444	927	(3,000)	4,371
1990	4,371	629	(5,000)	-0-
	$10,000	$5,000	$(15,000)	$ -0-

Unfortunately, an investment's IRR is not so simple to determine as these examples imply. It involves laborious trial-and-error computations. The IRR on an investment can be easily determined, however, through use of a calculator or computer program designed for that purpose.

Although IRR analysis is an invaluable tool for assessing the possible return on a proposed investment, it also has its limitations. For example, the IRR is the measure only of the return on the amount that *remains* invested. This is what the term "internal" in IRR means. Thus, although the IRR on the investment discussed previously is 14.38%, that rate is earned only on the amounts that remain invested — initially $10,000, then successively, $7,438, $6,508, $6,444 and $4,371. Unless the cash flows or withdrawals realized each year during the term of the investment can also be invested at 14.38%, the *terminal value*, or composite rate of return on the total transaction, falls below the IRR previously determined. For example, if the cash flows from the above example can be reinvested at an after-tax rate of only 8% (without withdrawal of principal or earnings), the terminal value IRR for the total investments falls from 14.38% to 11.67%. This can be demonstrated by the following analysis, which shows first the cash flow activity in the two investments over the five-year period.

Analysis of Cash Flows

	Original Investment				Secondary Investment			
Year	Beginning Amount Invested	14.38% Return	Cash With-Drawals	Ending Amount Invested	Beginning Amount Invested	8% Return	Amount Invested	Ending Amount Invested
1986	$10,000	$1,438	$ (4,000)	$7,438	$ -0-	$ -0-	$ 4,000	$ 4,000
1987	7,438	1,070	(2,000)	6,508	4,000	320	2,000	6,320
1988	6,508	936	(1,000)	6,444	6,320	506	1,000	7,826
1989	6,444	927	(3,000)	4,371	7,826	626	3,000	11,452
1990	4,371	629	(5,000)	-0-	11,452	916	5,000	17,368
	$10,000	$5,000	$(15,000)	$ -0-	$ -0-	$2,368	$15,000	$17,368

The buildup of the two investments, from a beginning balance of $10,000 to the ending balance of $17,368, reflects a composite or terminal value rate of return of 11.67%, as the following analysis shows.

Accumulation at 11.67%

Year	Beginning Amount Invested	11.67% Return	Ending Amount Invested
1986	$10,000	$1,167	$11,167
1987	11,167	1,304	12,471
1988	12,471	1,456	13,927
1989	13,927	1,626	15,552
1990	15,552	1,815	17,368
	$10,000	$7,368	$17,368

Another difficulty with using the IRR to analyze ROI arises when there is a *negative* cash flow (an additional investment) subsequent to the initial investment. Inherent in the IRR method is the requirement that all future cash flows, both positive and negative, be discounted to their present value at the same rate. This assumes that future negative flows, which must originate from outside the original investment, are provided from funds that have been earning the same rate of return as the amount originally committed to the investment. In more cases than not, that is an invalid assumption.

The problems caused by negative amounts in an investment's cash-flow stream do not impair the usefulness of ROI analysis. It is possible to factor out these negative amounts in ways that leave the integrity of the analysis unimpaired. There are various ways of doing so, all of which cannot be treated within the limited scope of this book. The following discussion, however, may provide some understanding of how this may be done.

Negative cash flow. A negative cash flow at some time during the term of an investment is basically no more than an additional investment requirement. It seems reasonable, therefore, to remove it from the cash-flow stream and consider it a part of the original investment. This serves to simplify the IRR analysis by leaving a cash-flow stream comprised only of positive amounts.

In removing a negative amount from a cash-flow stream and considering it instead as part of the original investment, a decision must be made as to the rate at which the future negative amount should be discounted to its present value. Stated another way, what is the amount that must be invested today to fund the future negative cash flow? As pointed out earlier, it cannot be assumed that the funding rate typically will be the same as the rate earned on the investment from which the negative cash flow arises. Accordingly, the *external* rate of return — the rate that can be earned outside the investment — should be used. Thus, an investor who has an external rate of return of 8% annually would have to set aside today $1,363 to satisfy a negative cash-flow requirement of $2,000 five years from now. This can be readily proved as follows.

Accumulation at 8% Annually

Year	Beginning Amount Invested	8% Return	Ending Amount Invested
1	$1,363	$109	$1,472
2	1,472	117	1,589
3	1,589	127	1,716
4	1,716	137	1,853
5	1,853	147	2,000

Having dealt with a negative cash flow in a proposed investment in the manner just described (sometimes called the "sinking fund" method), an investor can then move to an IRR analysis of the investment in the manner described above (see page 116).

Negative cash flows can be handled in ways other than the one described. For example, it can be assumed that negative cash flows are to be funded from the positive cash flows that immediately precede them rather than through an additional investment at inception. It is not so important *how* it is done; what *is* important is that the investor know that negative cash flows can be removed to prevent distortions in the results of an ROI analysis.

Perspective

Although the quantitative results of ROI analysis are invaluable aids to the decision-making process of tax shelter selection, an investor must keep the role of ROI analysis in its proper perspective. It is merely a tool, although an important one, and it cannot replace the essential role that knowledge, experience and judgment play in all investment decisions.

Glossary

This glossary contains many of the words and terms commonly encountered by investors in tax shelters. The definitions of such words and terms are intended to give the investor only a general understanding of their meaning; they are not intended to be technical or precise in a legal, accounting, tax or financial sense.

Abandonment Loss. In an oil and gas context, the cost of abandoned leases, equipment and other worthless property not previously deducted. A special allocation common to oil and gas partnership agreements allocates these costs to the limited partners.

Abusive Tax Shelter. An investment transaction devoid of any economic purpose other than the generation of tax benefits.

Accrual Method. A method of accounting that recognizes income and expense when all of the events have occurred to fix the right to receive the income or fix the fact of the liability, respectively, and the amount can be determined with reasonable accuracy.

Advance Royalty. Royalty payment made in advance of production of oil and gas, including lease bonus payments.

Alternative Minimum Tax. A minimum tax effective for years beginning after 1982. The AMT base is comprised of adjusted gross income (with some adjustments) plus various "tax preferences". That amount is reduced by certain deductions and by an exemption ($40,000 for married taxpayers filing joint returns; $30,000 for unmarried taxpayers); a tax rate of 20% is applied to the remainder. If the resulting tax amount exceeds the regular tax, the excess must be added to the regular tax to determine the total tax liability.

Amortization. The liquidation of a financial obligation on an installment basis; also, recovery of cost or value over a period of time.

Annual Constant (Loan Constant). The sum of 12 monthly payments expressed as a percentage of loan principal. For example, it takes $6 per month to amortize a $1,000 loan over 30 years at 6% interest. 12 times $6 equals $72, which is 7.2% of $1,000. The annual constant is therefore 7.2.

Appraisal. An estimate or opinion of value; a conclusion resulting from the analysis of relevant facts.

Amortization Schedule. A table showing the amounts of principal and interest due on a loan at regular intervals and the unpaid balance of the loan after each payment is made.

Appraiser. One qualified by education, training and experience to estimate the value of real and personal property, using experience, judgment, facts and formal appraisal processes.

Arbitrage. The simultaneous purchase and sale of the same security or its equivalent, with the expectation of profit from discrepancies in price.

Assumption of Mortgage. The taking of title to property by a grantee, whereby the grantee assumes liability for payment of an existing note secured by a mortgage or deed of trust against the property; the grantee thereby becomes a co-guarantor for the payment of the mortgage or deed of trust note. See Subject to Mortgage.

At-Risk Limitation (Investment Tax Credit). The tax law prevents certain taxpayers from claiming investment tax credit on amounts in excess of their economic investment, or on the amount that taxpayers have at risk of loss. Under certain circumstances, however, an investor is allowed the investment credit on amounts that exceed the amount at risk. Amounts at risk generally include investments of cash or other property and debt for which the taxpayer is personally liable (recourse debt).

At-Risk Limitation (Losses). Tax losses of certain taxpayers are limited to the amount the taxpayer has invested at risk of loss. Such amounts generally include investments of cash or other property and recourse debt. This loss limitation does not apply to investments in real estate.

Balloon Payment. The finals unequal installment payment on a note — greater than the preceding installment payments — that pays the note in full.

Banker's Acceptance. A draft or bill of exchange accepted by a bank which guarantees its payment.

Beneficiary. One entitled to certain economic benefits of a trust; one who receives profit from an estate, the title of which is vested in a trustee; the lender on the security of a note and deed of trust.

Blind Pool. A limited partnership that has not committed its resources to a specific property or project at the time of capital contributions by the limited partners.

Bridge Financing. A short-term loan for an interim period (usually from three to five years) beginning with the completion of a project and ending when long-term financing can be arranged, preferably at a lower rate.

Broker. Any person engaged in the business of effecting transactions for the account of others, but not including a bank.

Burned-Out Shelter. A tax shelter investment that has exhausted its tax advantages and has begun to generate taxable income without cash flow sufficient to pay the resulting tax.

Burnout. The point at which a tax shelter investment that has been generating tax losses begins to generate taxable income. Also referred to as "crossover" or "turnaround."

Call Option. An option to buy a specified good at a stated price during a stated period of time. See Put Option.

Capital Contribution. The amount contributed by an investor to a partnership to purchase a partnership interest. Such contributions generally include cash or other property, although they may include services.

Capitalization. An appraisal method that bases the value of property on its net income and an assumed rate of return on investment. The method usually entails the following steps:

☐ Determine net annual income.

☐ Select the appropriate capitalization (cap) rate (rate of return).

☐ Compute the value by dividing net income by the cap rate

Thus, property with an annual income of $30,000 would be valued at $500,000 using a cap rate of 6%, and at $428,500 using a cap rate of 7%.

Capitalization Rate (Cap Rate). A rate that is considered a reasonable rate of return on investment; it is used in the process of determining a value based on net income.

Carried Interest. A fractional interest in an oil and gas lease that by its terms relieves the holder from personal liability for a portion or all of the development and operating costs and permits the co-owners who assume such liabilities to recoup their expenditures out of the proceeds from the oil or gas produced and sold.

Carry. The cost of financing an acquisition of property, including interest, storage and insurance charges where appropriate.

Carved-Out Production Payment. A production payment assigned by the owner of an interest in oil and gas which is to be paid out of a fractional part of the owner's continuing interest. See Production (Oil) Payment.

Cash Distributions. Amounts paid by a partnership to its partners in accordance with the terms of the partnership agreement. These distributions ordinarily represent a return of investment and therefore are nontaxable to the recipient. When their cumulative total exceeds a partner's tax basis in the partnership, however, the excess normally will be taxable.

Cash Method. A method of accounting that recognizes income in the year actually (or constructively) received. Expenditures are deductible in the year actually paid.

Christmas Tree. An assembly of valves and fittings located at the casinghead of an oil well to control the flow of oil from the well to storage tanks or pipelines.

Closing Costs. Costs incurred in closing a real estate or other transaction, such as legal fees, escrow closing fees, title insurance costs, tax and other prorations, points paid on loans, etc.

Combination Program. An oil and gas partnership which drills a combination of exploratory and developmental wells.

Commissions. Amounts paid to syndicators for underwriting and directing the sale of limited partnership interests. Such costs are considered to be syndication expenses for tax purposes and must be capitalized rather than deducted.

Commitment. An agreement by a lender to make, buy or extend a mortgage loan; an agreement to acquire or sell real estate. The commitment by a lender specifies the conditions and terms that the borrower must meet by a certain time, beyond which the commitment is invalid. In the purchase or sale of real estate, the commitment specifies the consideration and other conditions of the sale.

Commitment Fee. A consideration paid by a mortgagor in return for a binding agreement to lend on a mortgage or to purchase property at a future date. It may or may not be refunded to the borrower when the loan is made or the property is purchased. The fee is retained by the lender as liquidated damages if the borrower fails to close the transaction.

Complete Payout (Oil and Gas). That point at which the gross income attributable to all of the operating mineral interests in an oil or gas property equals all expenditures for drilling and development of such property plus the cost of operating the property during the payout period. See Payout.

Condemnation. The act of taking private property for public use by a government unit; declaration that a structure is unfit for use.

Construction Loan. A loan, the proceeds of which are advanced during the construction period by prearrangement, to enable an owner to erect a new building. It is made generally on the strength of a firm commitment by an investor to purchase a permanent mortgage on the property after its completion.

Conversion. The result achieved by taking deductions against income taxable at ordinary rates and subsequently disposing of the asset from which the deductions arose in a transaction that results in a gain taxable at more favorable capital gain rates; sometimes described as the act of converting ordinary income into capital gain.

Cover. The offset of a previous futures transaction with an equal and opposite transaction.

Crossover. See Burnout.

Deep Shelter. A term used to describe a tax shelter that generates losses sufficient to offset unrelated taxable income.

Deferral. An investment strategy that results in delaying the payment of tax from one year to a later year. It is achieved by incurring expenses or losses that reduce current income otherwise taxable at maximum rates, with the expectation that such expenses or losses will be recouped in subsequent years under more favorable tax rates. In the interim, an economic benefit is realized from use of the funds that otherwise would have been used to pay taxes.

Delay Rentals. Amounts paid to a lessor under the terms of an oil and gas lease, subsequent to the payment of the bonus, for the privilege of deferring the commencement of a well.

Depletion. A deduction allowed for recovery of an investment in a wasting asset. Depending on the facts, the deduction may be based on the cost of the property or it may be measured by a percentage of the gross income from the property.

Depreciation. In an appraisal sense, a loss of property value through physical deterioration or functional or economic obsolescence; under the tax law, a deduction allowed for recovery of the cost of an asset.

Developmental Drilling. Drilling on a lease where reserves have been confirmed or proved by producing wells, in anticipation of production from the same reservoir; drilling on an offset lease in close proximity to a producing lease, in anticipation of production from the same reservoir. Although developmental drilling is less risky than exploratory drilling, there is no assurance that it will be successful.

Discount Bond. A bond, issued at or near par, which is currently selling substantially below par due to a rise in interest rates. Interest earned in the form of amortization of the discount is not taxed until the bond matures or is sold and then at capital gain rates.

Discounting. A method of computation used to determine the present value of a future stream or flow of cash. It requires assumptions of a desired rate of return and the timing of the future receipts. Thus, the present value of five successive annual payments of $1 beginning one year from today is $3.79, assuming a 10% annual rate of return. Stated differently, $3.79 invested today at 10% interest, compounded annually, will yield five successive annual payments of $1 beginning one year from today.

Dry Hole. A well that is nonproductive, that does not yield commercial quantities of oil or gas.

Economic Interest. Under income tax regulations, "an economic interest is possessed in every case in which the taxpayer has acquired by investment any interest in mineral in place or standing timber and secures, by any form of legal relationship, income derived from the extraction of the mineral or severance of the timber, to which he must look for a return of his capital." It is this interest in oil or gas in place which entitles the holder to a deduction for depletion on income derived therefrom.

Economic Life. The period over which a property will yield a return on investment.

Encumbrance. Anything that affects or limits the fee simple title to property, such as mortgages, easements or restrictions of any kind. Liens are special encumbrances which make the property security for the payment of a debt or obligation, such as mortgages and taxes.

Equity. The interest or value that an owner has in real estate or other property, over and above the liens against it.

Escalator Clause. A clause in a contract providing for the upward or downward adjustment of certain items to cover specified contingencies.

Exchange Offer. An offer by a corporation to exchange its stock for stock of another corporation or for other property. Such offers are sometimes made for limited partners' interests in a tax shelter partnership (usually one that has "burned out") in what is generally a nontaxable transaction. However, such transactions can be taxable to the extent a partner is relieved of obligations that exceed the tax basis of the partnership interest.

Ex-Dividend Date. The date a security on which a dividend has been declared sells without entitling the buyer to the dividend.

Exploratory Drilling. Drilling on unproved acreage in search of new reserves of oil or gas (sometimes called wildcat drilling). Also, an attempt to extend significantly the outer limits of a proved field, or drilling into deeper zones than those from which reserves are being produced.

External Rate of Return. The rate that can be earned on funds by the investor outside the current investment being considered, i.e., either on funds necessary for an additional contribution to such investment, or on tax savings generated by the investment. See Internal Rate of Return.

Farmout (Oil and Gas). Transfer of an oil and gas lease to secure its development. The assignor usually retains an overriding royalty interest, but may retain any type of interest or adjoining acreage.

Farmout (Loss). A transaction by which anticipated tax losses are transferred from a taxpayer who cannot use the losses with greatest advantage to a taxpayer who can. Safe harbor leasing transactions and research and development limited partnerships are, at least to some extent, farmouts of losses.

Fee. An estate in real property; the owner thereof is in absolute and legal possession.

Fee Simple. A fee that has no limitation to any class of heirs or restrictions on the transfer of its ownership.

Fiduciary. A person in a position of trust and confidence, such as that existing in real estate between principal and broker; as a fiduciary, a broker owes certain loyalty to the principal that cannot be breached under rules of agency.

Finance Lease. See Full Payout Lease.

Financial Forecast. An estimate of the most probable financial position, results of operations, and changes in financial position for one or more future periods. "Most probable" for this purpose means that the assumptions underlying the forecast represent management's judgment of the most likely set of conditions and its most likely course of action. (Compare to Financial Projection.)

Financial Projection. An estimate of financial results based on assumptions that are not necessarily the most likely. Financial projections are often developed as a response to such questions as "What would happen if. . .?" (Compare to Financial Forecast.)

Flip-Flop. That point at which special allocations of tax attributes between general and limited partners terminate; thereafter, the sharing of tax attributes reflects a new relationship between general and limited partners in which the general partners' profit-sharing percentage usually is increased substantially.

Footage Drilling Contract. A contract for the drilling of an oil or gas well that provides for payment at a specified price per foot for drilling to a specified depth.

Forward Contract. An agreement between two parties for the purchase/sale of a security, commodity or good in the future, under such terms as the parties agree on. Such contracts are not freely transferable and are not traded on organized markets.

Front-End Load. That portion of the capital contributed by investors that is absorbed by certain costs or fees such as management fees, syndication costs, legal fees, accounting fees, etc. Such costs are important to investors, since they reduce the amount that ultimately may be invested in assets that may produce income or gain.

Full Payout Lease. A lease structured to give the lessor full recovery of the cost and a reasonable return on the investment over the original noncancellable term of the lease; also called a finance lease.

Futures Contract. A standardized agreement for the purchase/sale of a security, commodity or good in the future. Unlike forward contracts, futures contracts are traded on organized markets.

General Partner. A partner in a limited partnership whose liability to partnership creditors is not limited. In a tax shelter partnership, the general partner normally is the person who "put the deal together" (or an entity controlled by this person); this is the partner responsible for control and management of the partnership's activities.

Graduated Lease. A lease that provides for a varying rental rate, with adjustments often based on factors to be determined in the future or on the result of periodic appraisals.

Gross Income. Total income from a property before deduction of any expenses.

Hard Costs. A term used in tax shelter transactions for those expenditures that result in the acquisition of an asset from which income or gain may be realized. In real estate, for example, the bricks and mortar used in construction are hard costs. See Soft Costs.

Hedge. A position taken opposite to one already held; its objective is to protect against losses that may occur through changes in price.

Highest and Best Use. That use of property (most commonly, real property) that is most likely to produce the greatest net return over a given period of time.

Income Multiplier (Yield Rate). A factor by which gross or net income from a property is multiplied to determine its probable value or selling price.

Intangible Drilling Costs (IDC). Those costs incurred in drilling an oil or gas well that in themselves have no salvage value; they must be "incident to and necessary for the drilling of wells and the preparation of wells for the production of oil and gas." Although such costs generally are deductible as paid or incurred, they may be "recaptured" as ordinary income in a taxable disposition of the property on which they were incurred.

Interim Financing. Temporary financing obtained during construction of a building pending the securing of a permanent mortgage.

Internal Rate of Return (IRR). The rate that will discount future cash flows from an investment to an amount that equals the amount invested; thus, it results in a net present value of zero. See External Rate of Return.

Investment Interest Limitation. A provision under the tax law that limits the deduction for interest paid to carry investments. Generally, the limitation is the sum of $10,000 plus net investment income.

Investment Tax Credit. A direct credit against income taxes that is allowed for investments made in certain business or investment property such as tangible, depreciable personal property with at least a three-year life and certain building rehabilitation costs.

Lease. A contract between an owner of property and a user, setting forth the conditions under which the user may possess and use the property and the term or period of the use.

Lease Bonus. Consideration paid for the grant or assignment of an oil and gas lease.

Legs. Positions held; this normally refers to long or short positions held in security or commodity futures contracts.

Lessee. One who contracts to use property owned by another under terms of a lease contract.

Lessor. An owner of property who contracts with another for its use under terms of a lease contract.

Letter of Credit. A financing transaction in which a bank issues to a borrower a letter authorizing the borrower to draw on the bank for a specified sum and guaranteeing to accept the drafts on the bank if they are made. Limited partners in tax shelter partnerships are sometimes required to obtain such letters, which may be used as security for partnership loans.

Leverage. The ability to acquire an asset with a minimum investment; the enhancement of purchasing power through borrowing. In real estate, for example, leverage is demonstrated in a transaction where the purchaser acquires a $1,000,000 property with a $250,000 down payment, the balance of $750,000 being financed by a mortgage loan secured by the property.

Leveraged Lease. A lease in which the lessor finances a portion of the leased property's purchase price with debt, usually nonrecourse debt.

Like-Kind Exchange. Exchange of property held for productive use in a trade or business or investment for property which is held either for productive use in a trade or business or for investment.

Limited Partner. A partner in a limited partnership whose liability to partnership creditors is limited to the amount of the partner's investment in the partnership, any additional amounts the partner may be obligated to contribute under terms of the partnership agreement, and the partner's share of undistributed partnership earnings. A limited partner may lose limited liability status by participating in the control of the partnership. See Limited Partnership.

Limited Partnership. A partnership formed by two or more persons, having as members one or more general partners and one or more limited partners. The limited partners as such are not bound by the obligations of the partnership. See Limited Partner.

Load. See Front-End Load.

Long. The purchase or ownership of a security, commodity or other property or a position therein. See Short.

Management Fee. A fee or compensation paid for services rendered in connection with the management of a business activity. In tax shelter partnerships, such fees may be paid to the general partner or to others and may be based on a percentage of gross rentals, an amount for each producing well, an amount for each piece of leased property, etc. Such amounts generally are deductible for tax purposes when paid or incurred.

Margin. Required equity an investor must deposit to collateralize an investment position.

Marginal Rate. The income tax rate that applies to the taxpayer's top dollar of taxable income.

Market Discount. The excess of the stated redemption price of the bond at maturity over the basis of the bond immediately after its acquisition by the taxpayer.

Mark-to-Market. Adjustment of the carrying value of an asset, such as a futures contract, to current market value.

Minimum (Guaranteed) Royalty. In oil and gas transactions, an obligation of a lessee to pay a lessor during the term of a lease either a fixed sum of money periodically or an agreed share of the proceeds of the oil or gas produced and saved, whichever is greater.

Minimum Tax. See Alternative Minimum Tax.

Negative Basis. A term sometimes used to describe the situation that results from claiming tax deductions from an activity that exceed the amount actually invested in the activity. It is a misnomer, however, since allowable tax deductions cannot exceed tax basis. The misunderstanding arises from investments made through the partnership form. Under certain circumstances, a partnership's liabilities are considered to be part of the partners' tax basis in the partnership. While this treatment may allow the partners to deduct losses that exceed their capital contributions to the partnership, it does not result in negative basis. This is a highly technical tax area that may confuse many investors, particularly in light of the at-risk rules that may deny tax losses. For example, some partnership liabilities may be considered a part of the partners' tax basis while failing to qualify as at-risk amounts that allow deduction of losses.

Net Lease. A lease arrangement under which the lessee is responsible for all expenses usually associated with property maintenance, including repairs, taxes, utility charges and insurance.

Nonrecourse Loan. A loan for which the borrower has no personal liability. Such loans may be secured by specific assets of the borrower. This is commonly the case in real estate financing transactions, where the lender may look only to the property itself as security for the loan.

Offering Memorandum. A document provided to potential investors in a tax shelter program. It normally contains information on the proposed investment, the terms and conditions under which it is offered, the risks involved, the federal tax consequences of the investment, financial projections, various information concerning the general partner and the general partner's relationship with the venture, etc. Also known as a "prospectus."

Operating Agreement. An agreement among the working interest owners of an oil and gas lease. The agreement designates one of the owners as the operator of the lease and spells out the rights and obligations of the operator and nonoperators.

Operating Lease. A short-term lease under which the lessor does not recover the cost of the leased property over the initial lease term. The risks are greater than the risks of a finance lease, since the lessor must either re-lease or sell the property profitably at the end of the initial lease term.

Operator. One who holds all or a fraction of the working or operating rights in an oil or gas lease and is obligated for the costs of production, either as a fee owner or under a lease or any other form of contract creating working or operating rights. See Working Interest.

Option. A contract right to buy or sell a security, commodity or other property.

Organization Costs. Costs incurred directly in the creation of a new business organization. Such costs include the cost of certain legal fees, accounting fees, organizational meetings, etc. Such costs generally are not deductible, but they may be amortized over a 60-month period beginning with the commencement of business.

Original Issue Discount (OID). The difference between market price and face value of a security when it is initially sold at less than face value by the issuer.

Overriding Royalty. An interest carved out of the lessee's working interest in an oil and gas lease entitling the holder to receive a fraction of production or the proceeds therefrom, free of any production or operating costs other than production, severance and windfall profit taxes.

Partnership. Generally, a legal relationship that has been created between two or more persons who contractually associate as joint principals in the conduct of a trade or business.

Payout. That point at which an amount invested has been recouped through cash distributions. It generally is accompanied by a reallocation of the rights to income or cash flow among the participants in an investment. See Complete Payout (Oil and Gas).

Percentage Lease. A lease under which the rental is determined by the amount of business done by the lessee; the rental is usually expressed as a percentage of gross receipts, but with provision for a minimum rental.

Phantom Income/Gain. Taxable income or gain that exceeds cash flow. Phantom income is realized when a tax shelter has "turned around" or "burned out." Phantom gain is realized when property is sold or otherwise disposed of for an amount sufficient only to satisfy the indebtedness against it.

Position. A market commitment, long or short, in a security or commodity. See Long, Short.

Pre-Opening Costs. See Start-up Costs.

Present Value. The value today of an amount due at a definite time in the future, determined by applying a selected discount rate to the future payment.

Private Offering. Generally, an investment offering that is not registered with the Securities and Exchange Commission. See Public Offering.

Production (Oil) Payment. A right to receive in cash or in kind a specified share of the production from a property until an agreed amount has been received. See Carved-out Production Payment, Reserved (Retained) Production Payment.

Profit-Sharing Ratio. The ratio in which partners have agreed to share profits and losses. Profit-sharing and loss-sharing ratios, however, sometimes differ.

Prospectus. See Offering Memorandum.

Public Offering. Generally, an investment offering that has been registered with the Securities and Exchange Commission. See Private Offering.

Purchase-Money Mortgage or Trust Deed. A trust deed or mortgage given as part or all of the purchase consideration for property. In some states, the only remedy for nonpayment of this type of mortgage is to foreclose on the property; there is no personal liability.

Put Option. An option to sell a specified good at a stated price during a stated period of time. See Call Option.

Recapture. The forfeiture, or recognition as ordinary income, of tax benefits previously allowed. Thus, investment tax credits may be forfeited, in whole or in part, if the property from which they arose is disposed of prior to the expiration of the required holding period. Likewise, gain on the sale or the disposition of certain property may be required to be returned as ordinary income (rather than as capital gain) to some extent if ordinary deductions have been allowed for depreciation or intangible drilling costs. Recapture of investment credits and certain losses also may be required because of the failure to meet certain at-risk rules that limit the use of credits and losses.

Refinancing. The repayment of existing debt from the proceeds of new borrowings.

Rehabilitation Costs. Costs incurred in the rehabilitation of certain buildings, for which the rehabilitation credit (see below) is allowed.

Rehabilitation Credit. A credit allowed for costs incurred in the rehabilitation of certain older buildings and certified historic structures. Depending on the age and status of the building, the credit may be 15%, 20%, or 25% of the rehabilitation costs.

Repurchase Agreement (REPO). An agreement that promises that securities will be bought back by the seller from the purchaser at a stated price.

Reserved (Retained) Production Payment. A production payment reserved or retained by the transferor of an interest in an oil or gas property. See Production (Oil) Payment.

Residual Value (Leasing). The expected value of the leased property at the end of the lease term.

Reverse Repurchase Agreement (Reverse Repo). An agreement that promises that securities will be resold to the original seller.

Royalty. The fraction of the oil or gas owned by a landowner or other holder of royalty rights. The holder of a royalty is entitled to receive a designated share of the proceeds from the sale of such oil or gas free of any production or operating costs excluding production, severance and windfall profit taxes.

S Corporation. A corporation that has gained, by election, a special status for tax purposes. It is treated somewhat (but not in all respects) like a partnership, since the results of its operations generally are reported by its stockholders and no tax is paid by the corporation. Qualification for such status is limited and accordingly not available to all corporations. Under recent changes in the tax law, the former Subchapter S corporation is now known as an S corporation.

Sale-Leaseback. A transaction in which the owner of property sells the property and leases it from the purchaser. The purposes of such a transaction vary; thus, the seller may enter into a sale-leaseback to realize appreciation that has built up in the property, or the transaction may be one in which the transfer of tax benefits is the primary consideration, such as in safe harbor leasing.

Section 8. A provision of the National Housing Act of 1959 for subsidizing the building of low-income housing. Investments in such housing offer certain tax and financing benefits that make them attractive to certain investors.

Section 1256 Contract. A contract that requires delivery of personal property or an interest in such property subject to a mark-to-market system traded on or subject to the rules of a domestic board of trade designated as a contract maker by the Commodity Futures Trading Commission.

Selling Expenses. Expenses incurred in marketing a tax shelter investment. Because such costs generally are paid from the investors' capital, their status for tax purposes is important. Certain costs, such as syndication costs, are not deductible for tax purposes.

Severance Tax. A state or local tax on the removal of minerals from the ground; usually levied as so many cents per barrel of oil or per MCF of gas, but it may be based on a percentage of value.

Short. The sale of, or position of, having sold a security, commodity or other property without ownership of such property at the time of sale. See Long.

Short-Against-The-Box. A short sale when the goods are already owned but will not be delivered against the sale until a later date.

Shut-In Royalty. A royalty paid to keep a lease alive without production from a well that is capable of production in paying quantities. Usually incurred in connection with gas wells that are shut-in for a lack of market.

Soft Costs. A term used in tax shelter transactions for expenditures that do not result in the acquisition of an asset from which income or gain may be realized. For example, administration expenses, sales commissions, management fees, etc. are soft costs. See Hard Costs.

Spread/Straddle. The simultaneous purchase and sale of option, security or commodity positions where the positions bought/sold are similar in kind but differ in price or delivery (expiration) date.

Spudding In. The very beginning of drilling operations in an oil or gas well.

Start-Up Costs. Costs necessary to starting a new business, incurred prior to commencement of active business operations. The extent of such costs and their status for tax purposes are important to an investor, since they may not be currently recoverable as tax deductions.

Subchapter S Corporation. See S Corporation.

Subject to Mortgage. The taking of title to real property subject to an existing mortgage, where the grantee is not responsible to the holder of the promissory note for the payment of any portion of the amount due. The most that grantee can lose in the event of a foreclosure is the grantee's equity in the property. See Assumption of Mortgage. In neither case is the original maker of the note released from responsibility on the debt.

Syndication. A joint venture, usually formed for one transaction and generally managed by one or a few of its members.

Syndication Expenses. Expenses incurred by a partnership in connection with the issuing and marketing of interests in the partnership. Examples of syndication expenses are brokerage fees; registration fees; legal fees of the underwriter or placement agent and the issuer (the general partner or the partnership) for securities advice and for advice pertaining to the adequacy of tax disclosures in the prospectus or placement memorandum for securities law purposes; accounting fees for preparation of representations to be included in the offering materials; and printing costs of the prospectus, placement memorandum, and other selling and promotional material. These expenses must be capitalized and cannot be recovered through amortization.

Take-or-Pay Contract. A gas-purchase contract requiring the purchaser to take a minimum annual volume of gas which the producer has available for delivery or, if the minimum volume is not taken, requiring the purchaser to pay for such minimum amount.

Tax Preference Items. Certain tax deductions and exclusions from income that have been selected for special treatment under the tax law. Depending on the extent to which they are used to reduce a taxpayer's taxable income, they may result in the imposition of the alternative minimum tax. Common preference items include the 60% exclusion on long-term capital gains and the deduction for accelerated depreciation in excess of straight-line depreciation.

Three-Corner Exchange. An exchange of property involving three parties, normally motivated by the desire of one party to secure the deferral of the recognition of gain accorded to exchanges of like-kind property. For example, Owner A has property, is willing to dispose of it, and wishes to acquire property held by Owner B. Since Owner A does not wish to recognize the gain that would result from a taxable disposition of the property, Owner A would like to exchange it for Owner B's property in a like-kind exchange. Owner B, however, will dispose of the property only for cash. Buyer C would like to acquire Owner A's property in a cash transaction. The objectives of all three parties can be satisfied by having Buyer C purchase Owner B's property for cash and then enter into an exchange of properties with Owner A.

Triple Net Lease. A lease transaction in which all expenses associated with the leased property, except for mortgage payments, are borne by the lessee; sometimes referred to as a net lease.

Turnaround. See Burnout.

Turnkey Drilling Contract. A contract for the drilling of a well that requires the driller to drill a well and, if commercial production is obtained, to equip the well to such a stage that the lessee or operator may turn a valve and the oil will flow into a tank.

Unit. The measure of participation in the ownership of a tax shelter investment. For example, a partnership seeking to raise $10,000,000 may offer to sell 1,000 units at $10,000 each. An investor may acquire one or more units. Minimums of more than one unit are often set by the partnership.

Variable Interest Rate Mortgage. A mortgage loan on which the interest rate increases or decreases in accordance with changes in some designated standard such as the prime interest rate.

Wash Sale. A sale of a security at a loss, followed by the purchase of a substantially identical security (or option to purchase a substantially identical security). If the substantially identical security is acquired within 30 days before or after the date of sale, the loss is not recognized for tax purposes.

Wildcat Drilling. See Exploratory Drilling.

Windfall Profit Tax. An excise tax imposed on most domestic crude oil. It is intended to prevent producers of crude oil from realizing windfall profits as a result of the deregulation of crude oil prices. See Appendix G for the tax rate structure.

Working Interest (Operating Rights). The interest in a mineral property evidenced by a lease or other form of contract. See Operator.

Wraparound Mortgage (All-Inclusive Deed of Trust). A purchase money deed of trust created when a seller conveys title to the buyer and takes back a mortgage in the amount of the entire unpaid purchase price, including the amount of any existing mortgages. The existing mortgages are not extinguished, and the seller is obligated to make the payments required on such obligations. The payments on the wraparound mortgage are usually sufficient for the seller to meet the payments on the pre-existing mortgages.

Zero-Coupon Bonds. Bonds or other evidences of indebtedness carrying no stated interest rate.

ACRS Cost Recovery Table — Personal Property

Personal Property Placed in Service After December 31, 1980

	Class of Investment			
Ownership Year	3-Year	5-Year	10-Year	15-Year Utility Property
	%	%	%	%
1	25	15	8	5
2	38	22	14	10
3	37	21	12	9
4		21	10	8
5		21	10	7
6			10	7
7			9	6
8			9	6
9			9	6
10			9	6
11				6
12				6
13				6
14				6
15				6
	100	100	100	100

ACRS Cost Recovery Table — Real Estate (Except Low-Income Housing)

Real Estate Placed in Service After March 15, 1984

Ownership Year	(Use the column for the month in the first year the property is placed in service)											
	1	2	3	4	5	6	7	8	9	10	11	12
	%	%	%	%	%	%	%	%	%	%	%	%
1	9	9	8	7	6	5	4	4	3	2	1	0
2	9	9	9	9	9	9	9	9	9	10	10	10
3	8	8	8	8	8	8	8	8	9	9	9	9
4	7	7	7	7	7	8	8	8	8	8	8	8
5	7	7	7	7	7	7	7	7	7	7	7	7
6	6	6	6	6	6	6	6	6	6	6	6	6
7	5	5	5	5	6	6	6	6	6	6	6	6
8	5	5	5	5	5	5	5	5	5	5	5	5
9	5	5	5	5	5	5	5	5	5	5	5	5
10	5	5	5	5	5	5	5	5	5	5	5	5
11	5	5	5	5	5	5	5	5	5	5	5	5
12	5	5	5	5	5	5	5	5	5	5	5	5
13	4	4	4	5	5	4	5	4	4	4	4	5
14	4	4	4	4	4	4	4	4	4	4	4	4
15	4	4	4	4	4	4	4	4	4	4	4	4
16	4	4	4	4	4	4	4	4	4	4	4	4
17	4	4	4	4	4	4	4	4	4	4	4	4
18	4	4	4	4	4	4	4	4	4	4	4	4
19	0	0	1	1	1	2	2	3	3	3	4	4
	100	100	100	100	100	100	100	100	100	100	100	100

The official table to be published by the Treasury Department may differ from the percentages shown above.

This table does not apply for short taxable years of less than 12 months.

ACRS Cost Recovery Table — Real Estate (Low-Income Housing)

Real Estate Placed in Service After December 31, 1980

Ownership Year	(Use the column for the month in the first year the property is placed in service)											
	1	2	3	4	5	6	7	8	9	10	11	12
	%	%	%	%	%	%	%	%	%	%	%	%
1	13	12	11	10	9	8	7	6	4	3	2	1
2	12	12	12	12	12	12	12	13	13	13	13	13
3	10	10	10	10	11	11	11	11	11	11	11	11
4	9	9	9	9	9	9	9	9	10	10	10	10
5	8	8	8	8	8	8	8	8	8	8	8	9
6	7	7	7	7	7	7	7	7	7	7	7	7
7	6	6	6	6	6	6	6	6	6	6	6	6
8	5	5	5	5	5	5	5	5	5	5	6	6
9	5	5	5	5	5	5	5	5	5	5	5	5
10	5	5	5	5	5	5	5	5	5	5	5	5
11	4	5	5	5	5	5	5	5	5	5	5	5
12	4	4	4	5	4	5	5	5	5	5	5	5
13	4	4	4	4	4	4	5	4	5	5	5	5
14	4	4	4	4	4	4	4	4	4	5	4	4
15	4	4	4	4	4	4	4	4	4	4	4	4
16			1	1	2	2	2	3	3	3	4	4
	100	100	100	100	100	100	100	100	100	100	100	100

This table does not apply for short taxable years of less than 12 months.

Cost vs. Benefit of Using Straight-Line Depreciation

Under the ACRS depreciation rules, a taxpayer may elect to use the straight-line method of depreciation for real estate rather than the accelerated rates provided in the ACRS recovery tables. Although such an election generally may be inappropriate for *residential* real estate, careful consideration should be given to whether the straight-line method should be elected for *nonresidential* real estate. This evaluation is essential because the use of the standard 18-year real property table will cause *all* accumulated tax depreciation to be recaptured as ordinary income upon the sale of a nonresidential property (to the extent of any gain), regardless of how long the property was held. By electing straight-line depreciation, *no* depreciation recapture is required, except for corporate taxpayers who must recapture 20% of the gain attributable to straight-line depreciation.

If it is anticipated that nonresidential real estate will be sold ultimately at a gain, consideration should be given to electing straight-line depreciation for that property. This decision will be influenced by the taxpayer's tax bracket, the amount of the gain that is anticipated on the sale, the taxpayer's cost of capital, and the period that the taxpayer anticipates that the property will be held. The difficulty of such a decision is compounded by the fact that it must be made conclusively for the year the property is placed in service, since the choice of life and method is irrevocable once the tax return for that year is filed.

The following table illustrates one means that might be used to decide between the accelerated and the straight-line depreciation methods. Using an internal rate of return analysis, the table plots the break-even point between accelerated and straight-line depreciation options at various assumed after-tax rates of return and holding periods. The analysis is based on the assumptions that depreciation deductions are used to reduce income otherwise taxable at the 50% rate and that capital gain is taxed at a rate of 20% upon sale of the property.

By referencing to the table, investor can readily determine the appropriate course of action. For example, the table shows that an individual taxpayer (in the assumed 50% tax bracket) who can earn an 8% after-tax return or incurs an 8% after-tax cost of capital should use the accelerated cost recovery method only if the taxpayer plans to hold the property for more than 25 years. (The insert in the table summarizes the points plotted along the break-even line.)

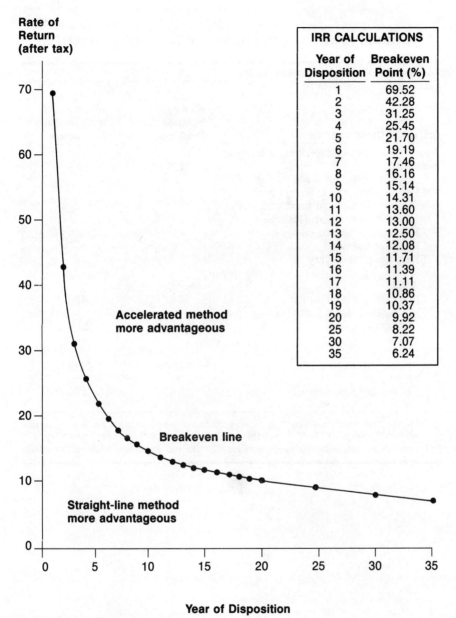

Rate of Return (after tax)

IRR CALCULATIONS	
Year of Disposition	Breakeven Point (%)
1	69.52
2	42.28
3	31.25
4	25.45
5	21.70
6	19.19
7	17.46
8	16.16
9	15.14
10	14.31
11	13.60
12	13.00
13	12.50
14	12.08
15	11.71
16	11.39
17	11.11
18	10.86
19	10.37
20	9.92
25	8.22
30	7.07
35	6.24

Accelerated method more advantageous

Breakeven line

Straight-line method more advantageous

Year of Disposition

● Breakeven line

Windfall Profit Tax Imposed on Domestic Crude Oil

Tax Imposed on Domestic Crude Oil

Crude Oil Classification	Tax Rate	
	All Except Independent Producers	**Independent Producers**
Tier 1 oil — all taxable domestic crude except:	70%	50%
□ oil from stripper wells		
□ oil in which the U.S. has an economic interest produced from a Naval Petroleum Reserve		
□ newly discovered oil		
□ certain heavy oil		
□ incremental tertiary oil		
Tier 2 oil:		
□ oil from stripper wells[1]	60%	0%
□ oil from a Naval Petroleum Reserve	60%	30%
Tier 3 oil:		
□ newly discovered oil[2]	22½%	22½%
□ heavy oil	30%	30%
□ incremental tertiary oil	30%	30%

1. Production from stripper wells by independent producers is exempt from tax, but only where daily production from a well has been 10 barrels or less for any consecutive 12-month period after 1972.

2. The tax rate on newly discovered oil will decrease to 20% in 1988, and to 15% in 1989 and thereafter.

Present Value Table

Present Value of $1 Due in 1 Through 20 Years at Selected Discount Rates

Year	8%	10%	12%	14%	16%	18%	20%
1	.92593	.90909	.89286	.87719	.86207	.84746	.83333
2	.85734	.82645	.79719	.76947	.74316	.71818	.69444
3	.79383	.75131	.71178	.67497	.64066	.60863	.57870
4	.73503	.68301	.63552	.59208	.55229	.51579	.48225
5	.68058	.62092	.56743	.51937	.47611	.43711	.40188
6	.63017	.56447	.50663	.45559	.41044	.37043	.33490
7	.58349	.51316	.45235	.39964	.35383	.31393	.27908
8	.54027	.46651	.40388	.35056	.30503	.26604	.23257
9	.50025	.42410	.36061	.30751	.26295	.22546	.19381
10	.46319	.38554	.32197	.26974	.22668	.19106	.16151
11	.42888	.35049	.28748	.23662	.19542	.16192	.13459
12	.39711	.31863	.25668	.20756	.16846	.13722	.11216
13	.36770	.28966	.22917	.18207	.14523	.11629	.09346
14	.34046	.26333	.20462	.15971	.12520	.09855	.07789
15	.31524	.23939	.18270	.14010	.10793	.08352	.06491
16	.29189	.21763	.16312	.12289	.09304	.07078	.05409
17	.27027	.19784	.14564	.10780	.08021	.05998	.04507
18	.25025	.17986	.13004	.09456	.06914	.05083	.03756
19	.23171	.16351	.11611	.08295	.05961	.04308	.03130
20	.21455	.14864	.10367	.07276	.05139	.03651	.02608

Computers in Tax Planning

Tax planning has long been an inseparable companion to sound financial planning. Although the immediate goal of such planning normally is to minimize current tax burdens, *effective* tax planning must reach further than the present. It must consider also the effect that present tax decisions may have on probable future tax positions. In doing so, planning must deal with the certainty of closed tax transactions and the likely tax results of other available transactions and their alternatives.

The increasing complexities of tax laws have placed a heavy burden on individuals who appreciate the value of tax planning in their overall financial plans. It now is almost physically impossible to accomplish that planning with the simple tools of pencil and ruled paper. The volume of calculations is too great; the effects of alternative courses of action are too pervasive; and the uncertain results of the intricate interactions of various tax attributes borders on intimidation. Fortunately, the microcomputer together with powerful tax planning software allows individual taxpayers to consider a wide variety of planning techniques and alternatives that would be impossible to explore on a manual basis.

The following summary of tax planning computer programs is representative of a variety of programs developed by Arthur Andersen & Co. in response to client needs for effective tax planning. They are included here to assure the tax shelter investor (who needs effective tax planning perhaps most of all) that effective tax planning tools are available to cope with the question of how tax shelter investments may affect present and future tax positions. In today's tax environment, that is no small comfort.

TAXCOM™ *calculates individual income taxes for taxable years 1982 through 1999. The program applies all available methods for determining tax liability, including income averaging and alternative minimum tax, and selects the optimum method. Reports show all calculations for all methods. Operates on the microcomputer.*

Features

☐ Computes breakeven point between alternative minimum tax and lowest of the other results.

☐ Analyzes income brackets, allowing you to enter a range of values for a given item and display the effect of all values in the range on the taxpayer's income bracket.

☐ Identifies effective marginal tax brackets for each determinant of liability.

☐ Produces a two-dimensional graph showing the points of bracket change for changes in an item of income or deduction.

☐ Allows you to display individual tax calculations, change one or more input item and instantly recompute tax liability.

☐ Provides an audit trail of tax calculations.

```
04/23/84              TAXCOM - Data Editing          8:57 AM

YEAR OF CALCULATION          1983
FILING STATUS                   3       To change a value, move the
1982 TAXABLE INCOME        200000       cursor to the desired line
1981 TAXABLE INCOME        150000       using the up-cursor (or F1 key)
1980 TAXABLE INCOME        175000       and down-cursor (or F2 key).
1979 TAXABLE INCOME        140000       When the cursor is on the line
ORDINARY INCOME            220000       to be changed, type the new
NET CAPITAL GAIN            60100       value, followed by return.
MEDICAL                     3000        When all changes have been
CASUALTY LOSSES             5000        made, position the cursor on
STATE AND LOCAL TAXES      20000       'DISPLAY REPORT' and press the
CHARITABLE CONTRIBUTIONS    4000        return key.
INTEREST DEDUCT FOR REG AND AMT  80000
INTEREST DEDUCT FOR REG ONLY     20000
OTHER ITEMIZED DEDUCTIONS    4000
EXEMPTIONS                   2000
OTHER PREFERENCES           20000   Adj. Gross Income      244,040
CREDITS AVAIL FOR REG AND AMT    0  Taxable Income         117,440
```

EXECALC *projects a taxpayer's federal and state tax liability and cash flow for up to ten years. A spreadsheet system model, it operates on the microcomputer.*

Features

☐ Projects the taxpayer's federal tax liability for each year of the projection period, applying income averaging when applicable and arriving at the lowest tax.

☐ Calculates and applies the alternative minimum tax where applicable.

☐ Calculates the investment interest expense limitation for regular tax purposes, and calculates the interest expense limitation for alternative minimum tax purposes.

☐ Projects annual cash flows for each year of the projection, and displays annual and cumulative cash flows at three different user-entered present value rates.

☐ Details the projection of itemized deductions, capital gains and losses, charitable contributions and partnership income and expenses.

☐ Allows user to define state tax computations to customize the template to any particular state. State tax options range from simply entering a state tax liability to calculating state taxable income from federal entries and user-defined adjustments, then computing tax based on user-entered tax tables.

☐ Permits insertion of lines into the basic model to adapt it to specific client situations.

SHELPLAN *is a microcomputer spreadsheet model used to analyze a tax shelter investment. It projects cash flow and taxable income from a specific investment for up to 11 years. SHELPLAN's primary use is to model the economics of an investment in a real estate limited partnership. In addition to allowing a user to change assumptions quickly and see the effects of changes, the system produces schedules that are suitable for inclusion in an offering memorandum.*

Features

☐ Reports show annual cash flow and taxable income for the partnership as a whole and for an individual partner.

☐ Shows after-tax benefit and rate of return of the investment to the individual partner.

☐ Calculates mortgage amortization for three mortgages, those with interest-only terms, and those with balloon payments.

☐ Calculates depreciation, investment tax credit, and preferences.

☐ Considers the effect of selling a limited partnership unit in the final year of projection.

☐ Calculates tax effects by applying user-supplied rates for ordinary income and capital gains.

☐ Calculates amortization, including construction period interest and taxes.

☐ Updated for 1984 Tax Act.

CASHFLOW *calculates the internal rate of return and/or the present value of an uneven cash stream. It provides a convenient way to enter repeating cash flows and accepts annual, quarterly or monthly data. Operates on the microcomputer.*

Features

☐ Calculates multiple present values when present value percentage is entered with a minimum, a maximum and an increment.

☐ Computes all internal rates of return for each cash stream.

☐ Displays proofs of all calculations.

☐ Graphs the internal rate of return, comparing rate against present value.

☐ Calculates present value and rate of return on uneven cash flows; to calculate these on even cash flows, use the INTEREST program.

```
PRESENT VALUES

A. SUMMARY

     ANNUAL RATE      PRESENT VALUE
        10.000%          $2,274.42
        15.000%            $921.24
        20.000%           -$239.87
        25.000%         -$1,295.66
        30.000%         -$2,091.07


THE POSSIBLE INTERNAL RATES OF RETURN ARE:
    18.90212997801025 %
   -33.73290000836791 %

PROOF OF INTERNAL RATE OF RETURN


1. PROOF OF 18.90213 % ANNUAL INTERNAL RATE OF RETURN COMPOUNDED  1  TIMES PER YEAR:

        -END OF-      BEGINNING        18.9021                              ENDING
        YEAR SEG       BALANCE        INTEREST      INVESTMENTS   WITHDRAWALS    BALANCE

            0            0.00            0.00       10,000.00         0.00      10,000.00
            1        10,000.00        1,890.21            0.00    -2,500.00      9,390.21
            2         9,390.21        1,774.95            0.00    -1,000.00      8,165.16
            3         8,165.16        1,543.39            0.00    -3,500.00      6,208.55
            4         6,208.55        1,173.55            0.00         0.00      7,382.10
            5         7,382.10          620.39            0.00    -4,750.00       -847.51
            6          -847.51         -160.20            0.00    -5,300.00     -6,307.71
            7        -6,307.71       -1,192.29        7,500.00         0.00        -0.00


2. PROOF OF -33.7329 % ANNUAL INTERNAL RATE OF RETURN COMPOUNDED  1  TIMES PER YEAR:

        -END OF-      BEGINNING        -33.733%                             ENDING
        YEAR SEG       BALANCE        INTEREST      INVESTMENTS   WITHDRAWALS    BALANCE

            0            0.00            0.00       10,000.00         0.00      10,000.00
            1        10,000.00       -3,373.28            0.00    -2,500.00      4,126.72
            2         4,126.72       -1,392.06            0.00    -1,000.00        245.34
            3          -245.34           89.51            0.00    -3,500.00     -3,675.83
            4        -3,675.83        1,239.96            0.00         0.00     -5,535.87
            5        -5,535.87        2,204.73            0.00    -4,750.00     -9,081.14
            6        -9,081.14        3,063.32            0.00    -5,300.00    -11,317.82
            7       -11,317.82        3,817.82        7,500.00         0.00         0.00
```

Index

W–X–Y–Z